Praise for "Bee Club Basics"

"The (Bee Club Basics) book was here when I landed home. THANK YOU THANK YOU and PS: thank you for doing it in larger print!!!!!!!!!!!!!!!!!!!!!! Next time we meet coffee is on me!"

— Kit S. July 22, 2021

"Charlotte Ekker Wiggins, author of two books about beekeeping and beekeepers, is our guest today. Her first book, **Bee Club Basics, Or How To Start A Bee Club***, dealt with managing teachers mentors, students, classes and the basics of organizing a start-up beekeeping organization. Her second book....***A Beekeeper's Diary: Self Guide To Keeping Bees***. [Late breaking news! "A Beekeeper's Diary" just won a Bronze Award in the Home & Garden Category from the Independent Publisher Book Awards! Congratulations Charlotte!]....Check out both of Charlotte's books. They are different enough from what you have that it will be worth your time."*

— Kim Flotum, *Beekeeping Today Podcast, June 14, 2021*

"What a game changer, all of my questions about how to start a bee club were in this book. Not to mention saving me a first trip to the lawyer's office to get started. Thank you, this is a great help. I owe you one or a dozen!"

— Joe K. April 2, 2021

"This is one of the most organized and detailed reference books I have come across.... With easy-to-read pages and over 30 pages of references and resources, her book covers all the basics needed to feel confident starting a local club."

— Carol Hrusovszky, *American Bee Journal, June 2020*

Wonderful Book - Great Info - Not just for Bee Clubs

"This book gives you useful information in an easy to understand entertaining format. Charlotte is a wonderful teacher. The structure of the information would

work for any club that wants to get off to a good start and avoid some of the pitfalls of starting from scratch. It includes sample agendas, checklists, surveys, class certificates, useful resources with website links, and 28 pages of pullouts that we are allowed to copy for use with our own clubs. Interspersed throughout are conversation bubbles of interesting facts about bees. There is also a glossary of beekeeping and other terms that help the beginner understand some of the referenced activities or topics."

Amazon Verified Purchaser Review March 1, 2020

A Very Practical Guide

"...In simple, easy to read print, this book covers all the pieces of the "club" organization process. Even with no previous experience, a group of interested, dedicated beekeepers can organize a club. It covers everything from advertising to volunteers in "how-to" fashion. It includes handy lists which provide step-by-step instructions that will lead to forming a well-organized and smooth-running club. An additional nice feature is that some pages are designed to be removed and copied for use by many. So, if you want to move from "coffee-club" to a member supportive, perhaps even community supportive organization, this is the book for you."

Amazon review February 6, 2020

A bunch of great information in one book!

"If you are interested in starting a beekeeping club, this is the book for you! It also has a lot of bee knowledge for those who just want to learn about bees in general. Very easy to read! Highly recommend!"

Amazon Verified Purchaser Review February 2, 2020

A Must-Have for the Leaders of Bee Clubs—New or Established

"...Leadership changes. I have found his book to be a valuable reference for leaders of already existing local bee clubs. It will give them new ideas and help keep their organizations tuned-up and operating efficiently and effectively."

—Gregg Hitchings, *Belleview Valley Apiary, January 31, 2020*

BEE CLUB BASICS

or HOW TO START A BEE CLUB

SECOND EDITION

Charlotte Ekker Wiggins

Bee Club Basics: How to Start a Bee Club, Second Edition

Copyright © 2022 by Charlotte Ekker Wiggins, LLC

All rights reserved. This book or any portion thereof may not be reproduced or used in any manner whatsoever without the express written permission of the publisher except for the use of brief quotations in a book review.

All photos by, and property of the author, unless otherwise identified.

Printed in the United States of America

First Printing 2019
Second Edition 2022

ISBN: 978-1-7357319-3-3 (Trade Paperback)
ISBN: 978-1-7357319-5-7 (Print Replica eBook)

Published by: Charlotte Ekker Wiggins, LLC | Rolla, MO | CharlotteEkkerWiggins.com

For more information contact: 4charlottewiggins@gmail.com

Cover Illustration: J. Tupper
Cover Design and Interior Formatting: Becky's Graphic Design®, LLC

ON THE COVER:

Honey bees (Apis mellifera) among Red Crimson Clover (Trifolium incarnatum) which provides early spring nitrogen as a cover crop, helps recondition soil and is an excellent nectar and pollen source. Not to be confused with Red Clover (Trifolium pretense) which has **round flower heads** *that are too long for honey bee tongues to reach the nectar.*

Dedication

To my lovely honey bees, who work together so diligently for the benefit of the whole colony. Let's take our cue from them and work together for the better health of our mutual home: EARTH.

~ Charlotte

Acknowledgments

Hugs to my brothers David and Stephen Ekker who offered advice and suggestions. I wouldn't dare include most of them but they kept me laughing.

A toast with a cold mug of beer to my "bee buddy" David Draker who February 2014 innocently volunteered to "help" when a number of beginning beekeeping students asked me to start a bee club. He's been my partner in beekeeping since then including teaching classes, chasing swarms and talking bees. Make that talking A LOT about bees.

A nice start of sweet yellow clover for my gardening buddy Tom Miller. I won't mention how many times he sat through our beginning beekeeping classes. He has proven to be an excellent student and an even better beekeeping mentor and coach. He still beats me to some of the area plant sales. Darn it.

Large honey jar to J. Tupper. I met J. through the April 11, 2019 Missouri S&T TEDx and the charming graphics she drew for the 9 speakers featured in that event including me. She is such a talented artist with a great sense of humor. And now she knows more about honey bees, too!

Grateful for the advice of James Crump, an attorney who solemnly nodded every time I said let's keep this simple. And did.

Appreciation for the input of Sheila Flint, an accountant who volunteered suggestions to keep the money lines clean without even being asked.

A front yard full of "noxious weeds" to Michele Colopy, LEAD for Pollinators, Inc. who kindly gave this second edition a sanity check. I suspect she will also be tickled to be following an attorney and accountant who were also tapped for book information. She's already said she will be glad to be a follow-up resource for you. **https://leadforpollinators.org**

Thankful to Hannah Ewart and her feline assistant Staci for the last manuscript proofing before I sent it on to the book designer — amazing the things that escaped me.

Sweet gratitude for the work of Becky Bayne and Kayla Swedberg, **BeckysGraphicDesign.com** who turned this into a visually interesting and easy to use paperback and ebook. I will make beekeepers of them yet!

Best wishes to those club leaders who have reached out since the first edition and inspired me to add new sections and topics to this second edition. Hope these ideas and suggestions help you help beekeepers in your communities.

Contents

Dedication iii

Acknowledgments iv

Contents v

Here's the Buzz vi

Chapter 1: Why Establish a Bee Club 1

Chapter 2: Basic Bee Club Structures 15

Chapter 3: How to Pay Bills 23

Chapter 4: Organizing a Bee Club 31

Chapter 5: Getting "Paperwork Organized" 45

Chapter 6: Bee Club Leadership 65

Chapter 7: Conflicts of Interest 83

Chapter 8: Managing Bee Club Volunteers 89

Chapter 9: Monthly Bee Club Programs 101

Chapter 10: Special Bee Club Events 111

Chapter 11: Getting the Word Out 139

Chapter 12: Meeting Online 155

Chapter 13: Changing Laws 161

Chapter 14: Working Partnerships 169

Chapter 15: Stepping Away 177

Chapter 16: Bee Club References 189

Chapter 17: Sample Check Lists and Documents 199

About the Author 253

Other Published Works 254

Glossary of Terms 257

Index 263

Here's the Buzz

Missouri, like many other states across the country, has seen the number of local bee clubs increase from six a decade ago to more than 48 bee clubs December 2021. The challenge is that many of those clubs are looking for help, from how to set themselves up and how to be sustainable to how, and what, to discuss at meetings, especially amidst a worldwide pandemic. Since the first edition of "Bee Club Basics" was published October 2019, dozens of associations and club leaders have contacted me for my lecture on **how to start, and reinvigorate, bee clubs** followed by lengthy question and answer sessions as well as private discussions.

This second edition **provides help for both new and established bee clubs,** as much to provide a starting point as well as encouragement and support. Some of the basic bee club structure elements have been expanded to include the various nonprofit designations as well as the difficult concept of conflict of interest. I also cover the harder-to-find aspects of any club organization and management, with suggested ways to deal with them. This is not all-inclusive, it is a practical guide to the key elements to start, and re-start, an educational nonprofit bee club.

Although this blueprint is focused on "bee clubs," the **principles apply to any group** trying to establish an educational nonprofit that supports their interests.

Some of these suggestions are based on my personal experience establishing more than a dozen nonprofit charitable clubs since 1979. I also retired from public affairs careers with USDA Forest Service and US Navy and currently still manage a custom gift business. I share tips from those parts of my life to help make you more effective in how manage a nonprofit business and share information, which can be challenging all on their own.

Just so that you can also see what some of the guide advice looks like in action, take a look at **RollaBeeClub.com.** I founded and am currently one of the planning team members for this educational nonprofit started in 2014 at the request of beekeeping students who wanted a local club to support their beekeeping journey.

I have also tapped, and incorporated, suggestions from Michele Colopy, Leadership, Education, Action, Development (LEAD) for Pollinators, Inc. an excellent nonprofit in its own right designed to help beekeepers. Start with her blog which is an excellent source for ongoing club management issues: https://leadforpollinators.org/our-blog/ You bet you can tell her I sent you.

This guide is approved by the Great Plains Master Beekeeping Program (GPMB) University of Nebraska at Lincoln, for Journeyman level training. It is also a stand alone guide.

Please let me know how this guide works for you. If you have additions or suggestions, pass them along to 4charlottewiggins@gmail.com so I can include them in future updates.

If I have one piece of advice, it is to get a **group of reliable, trustworthy people** who back each other up. If you organize for the right reason, other people with similar views will find you.

Happy bee club keeping!

Charlotte

My Those Are Big Letters

Have you ever picked up a book on management or, worse yet, some sort of a legal guide? The letters are tiny, the easier to make them obscure, according to my bee buddy David.

I wanted this to be an **easy to access reference guide** and that includes being able to easily read the pages.

I made the letters larger so that we can all read this in the setting where we normally go through these kinds of books — bedtime. Now you should be able to get through - a couple of pages - be-fore you...fall...(sweet dreams!)

Your Notes

CHAPTER 1

Why Establish a Bee Club

"To make a prairie it takes a clover and one bee, One clover, and a bee, And revery. The revery alone will do, If bees are few."
— *Emily Dickinson, (1830-1886) American poet*

With one out of every three bites of food we eat courtesy of mostly honey bees, getting a group of beekeepers together regularly is **critical to any beekeeper's success.** Having a place to share challenges and get helpful suggestions is now a prerequisite to successful beekeeping. Between the impacts of pesticides, pathogens carried by *Varroa destructor* mites, poor nutrition and lack of foraging sources, **today's beekeeper is even more dependent** on their local beekeeping community to stay on top of recent developments and successful strategies.

One way beekeepers stay in touch is by getting together. This can be as simple as having coffee at the same time every few weeks and tends to be how beginning bee club organizers envision their club. Let's face it, who in their right mind would choose to take on the paperwork a formal bee club requires?

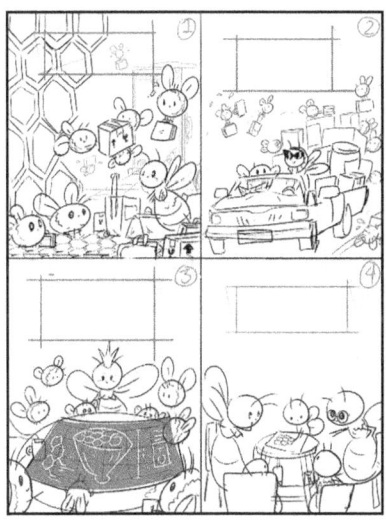

*This was one of the first drawings for the concept of this book cover. You may also have **several versions of meetings** before you settle on how you want to meet. Stay flexible, keep your focus on your goal and have coffee handy!*

PURPOSE OF A BEE CLUB

At a time when we are more electronically connected than ever, studies show that as a **society we are feeling more alone than ever.** What's missing? It's the age-old yearning to be accepted, to spend time with others – that's the revery part - and still share. It's the basis of living together as a community, especially in the middle of a worldwide pandemic.

So **how do we get people together?**

COMMON GOALS AND BASIC NEEDS

Make it about, and include, them.

There's a tendency sometimes for a new club to think they need one expert guru who has all of the answers. Or another frequent club structure is to only bring in outside speakers, overlooking what local expertise may be available. It's good to have expert resources but let's start simple with your potential club members. **Who are they? What do they want? What can they offer?**

If you are getting people together to discuss getting a bee club started, what do you want? Make it measurable so you can gauge progress. And **don't let this all** fall on your shoulders. For example, if you are establishing a group that does something more than exchange stories, encourage people to bring in their samples, and examples, and have them share. Not everyone is comfortable speaking in front of a group so **ask them before hand;** sometimes the early ask leads to participation. If they know what is expected, they have time to prepare and are more apt to agree.

Getting others involved early sets the tone that **this is a team.**

MAKE IT ENJOYABLE

I know it is easy to become regimented and preachy but try to remember why you are getting together; you **want people to come back!** Make it **welcoming, entertaining and enjoyable.** Think more of this as being a family you are creating and plan the meetings more like a family reunion.

And don't forget the all-important rallying point. Our club was attending a state-sponsored first ever field day and the first question I was asked was where was the coffee. If there is one easy thing you can do to bring people together, it is to **have the coffee ready!**

HONEYBEES OR HONEY BEES

Believe it or not, at one time a bee club spent a good amount of time in a meeting discussing the merits of how to spell this word so let me tackle this right off the bat.

According to the Entomological Society of America, when a species is a true example of a particular taxon, that taxon is written separately. In other words, *Apis mellifera* is a distinct bee species so references to it should be spelled out in **two words.**

BASIC "GET TOGETHER" NEEDS

Even simple get-togethers require structure and can set the tone for follow up and support. There will be enough buffering along the way as you try to settle into a meeting format so try to get these basics worked out first:

Someone to **find a location** and/or an online meeting application;

- Set up **a date;**
- **Notify** interested parties;
- **Arrange room** layout and seating.
- If meeting online, you need people who know **how to run** the online meeting software.
- Regardless of in person or online, someone needs to **plan a program** and, inevitably,
- That person tends to become the fall back for planning future meetings.
- What if something happens in the meeting planners' personal life, in their professional careers and now there is no one to get some of the work done? Or better yet, how many of you have started on this path only to find yourselves **holding a meeting space rental bill** no one else has helped to pay?

SPEND TIME PLANNING

The process of "getting together" does not have to be challenging but it does require advance planning, setting early expectations, being accountable and being consistent in the follow through. Ask yourselves, and it should be more than one person doing this: **what is the purpose of getting together?**

If the answers are that you just want to get together to drink coffee and swap beekeeping stories, enjoy. You don't need a formal bee club structure to support a group of people regularly socializing.

However, if you are wanting to develop a **network of people** who support each other, work together and make themselves available to help each other become better beekeepers, something **akin to the superorganism** that is a bee colony, that is more like **creating a family and community.** A bee club is one of the ways you can build that support, share the workload and still have that cup of coffee.

WHAT DO YOU WANT TO DO

Think about what happens when your family starts talking about taking a vacation. Some people say no, they can't, others insist they have to, then there is the joy of arguing over where to go, what to do, how much to spend…The point is, a group of you interested in getting a club together need to agree that **first, you want a club,** and secondly then **sort out the details** of what kind of club. You want your planning team to have the **same picture of the future** so you're all working in the same direction.

- When I start a club, I ask what is it that we as a group want to do. **Focus on the team approach** or you will end up being the only person who does it all.

- Some people struggle with this so ask how they would **imagine a club 10 years from now**- what is the club doing, who are their members, what all is going on.

- Once you start finding common elements, you are starting to develop goals. Goals are **what you want the club to be.** You know you are starting with little so the work is in that "in between" part. Don't have more than three goals; one is fine. The idea is to **focus your energy on the same goals** that will get you where you want to end up.

HOW TO GET THERE

After settling on what your goals are, **talk about how to get there.** The steps you plan to take should be

- Specific,
- Measurable,
- Have goal dates and
- Specify who will do each step.

You can **adjust those dates** as you go along but putting a date on anything **makes it more realistic.** It also gives you **measurable progress** and that's important when you are starting – well, anything, really- but in particular something like a new club. People want to **see progress** once everyone decides what you are going to do.

WHAT WILL IT TAKE

Finally you will need to sort through what **specific actions** you are going to take. And here's the good news. If you have your goals and objectives clearly defined, you can **discard suggestions** that won't get you where you want to end up and you can focus only on those things that will work.

Many groups skip these steps and end up spinning their wheels. Remember most people have a lot of ideas and suggestions; focus on those ideas and suggestions people want to pursue. The challenge is how to get them **consistently and sustainably implemented.**

WRITE IT OUT

Once you have specific goals and tasks identified, write them out. Be specific about what the goal is and goals are; if you need specialized talents and equipment, note that. You want others to be able to read and agree with that you want to accomplish.

Same thing with tasks. Write them down, put names, delivery dates, specific needs—on paper. It's amazing how many things we each have in our minds but they don't get translated to others. Writing it out will do so. And you will have a record to look at back a few years later to note what progress you've made.

SAMPLE PLANNING CHART

WHAT YOU WANT TO DO, HOW DO YOU PLAN TO DO IT

	GOAL 1	GOAL 2	GOAL 3	NOTES
Describe goals				
How to implement				
What action				
What desired result(s)?				
By whom (name) someone responsible				
What needed (list supplies/actions)				
By when (set a goal date)				
What happens if goal not met (describe impact)				
Other needed measurable steps				

HOW TO KEEP HONEY BEES

Regardless of what approach you decide to take, let's tackle one of the most-asked questions, **how aspiring and new beekeepers who may be forming a club can talk about keeping bees.** Yes, it will be helpful to have experienced beekeepers helping you but there are also **excellent best management practice guides** to give you a start.

For example, these are the curated suggested best management practices from Missouri State Beekeepers Association. I was among the group of beekeepers with more than 200 years of beekeeping experience among them who developed these. What I like about these is that they are a **succinct outline** of what good beekeepers today should be doing. I use these in my beginning beekeeping classes as a **short version of how to successfully keep bees.** Although this is from Missouri's State Beekeepers Association, the principles apply to anyone keeping bees in the US today.

Missouri State Beekeepers Association's Best Management Practices for Missouri Beekeepers (Updated September 24, 2020)

INTRODUCTION

The Missouri State Beekeepers Association (MSBA) has developed and offers the following best management practices as suggestions for people who currently keep, or are thinking about, keeping (honey) bees in Missouri. Show-Me beekeepers note:

   a. MSBA intends for these to be concise "suggestions" of what to do, not a detailed explanation of how or why to do it. Details are readily available through other sources. Some links to MSBA-reviewed and MSBA-endorsed information are provided.

   b. Many of these practices will be recognized as common sense steps in being a "good neighbor" or pertain to keeping bees in an urban environment.

   c. Following these management practices will provide benefits to the beekeeper, his/her apiary and the surrounding community while reducing potential conflicts.

d. Things change. MSBA will revise and edit this list of best management practices as new information becomes available and changes are warranted.

Recommended practices for maintaining honey bee colonies in Missouri include:

1. Make an informed decision before committing to the start-up expense and responsibility of keeping bees. Do your **research, take a class and visit with area beekeepers.** Seek out a mentor.
2. **Read and understand** all laws, regulations and ordinances which may apply to keeping bees in your specific area.
3. **Keep healthy (honey) bees.** By that, we mean:
4. Keep bees only in well maintained Langstroth, top bar or other appropriate hives designed **with removable frames** allowing proper inspection and management of the individual combs of the colony.
5. Become familiar with pests and diseases which can affect your (honey) bees. A very good resource, **Honey Bee Diseases and Pests,** has recently been developed by the University of Minnesota. This guide provides information concerning the identification of honey bee diseases and pests, along with currently recommended treatment options.
6. Provide **regular hive inspections** for disease and strive to maintain strong active colonies by monitoring *varroa* mite and small hive beetle populations and taking appropriate action when necessary.
7. Obtain (honey) bees from a **trusted source.** If buying an established colony, make certain it is inspected for disease and mite loads prior to purchase.
8. **Be wary of used equipment "bargains,"** especially with woodenware.
9. *Varroa* mite monitoring and control is best accomplished utilizing information provided by the Honey Bee Health Coalition. Check out: **Tools for *Varroa* Management-A guide to Effective *Varroa* Sampling & Control.**
10. If a colony's population begins diminishing for an unknown reason, take immediate action:

    a. Reduce the entrance so the remaining bees can better guard against robbing.

    b. Then research and/or seek help from others to identify the problem.

11. **Properly treat** with a product approved for the specific conditions of concern, following all label instructions, or remove and destroy all diseased and/or pest infested colonies.

12. A diagnosis of **American foulbrood** should be **taken very seriously** as it generally is always fatal to the colony and readily spreads to others. Frames and combs should be burned and remaining woodenware scorched.

13. Always do a **thorough health check** on any colonies from which you wish to make splits or before combining colonies.

14. **Rotate one third of the oldest brood comb** out of the apiary each year.

15. Take **measures to reduce drifting and robbing** within your apiary.

    a. Quick action is necessary to keep robbing activity from spreading mites and potential pathogens in your apiary and those of other beekeepers in the area.

    b. By taking quick action, the woodenware and comb can be spared the ravages of the wax moth and small hive beetle. Procrastination will lead to a loss of time and beekeeping resources. Guaranteed!

16. **Humanely dispatch** any remaining live (honey) bees by **shaking/brushing into soapy water.**

17. Place frames and combs **in a freezer for 24 hours** prior to reuse or storage to kill larvae of the small hive beetle and wax moths.

18. Practice proper management and control techniques to prevent colonies from swarming.

19. Maintain all colonies **at least 10 feet away** or the minimum distances required by any local ordinances from property lines.

20. Placement in full sun or in areas of minimal shade can be helpful in reducing issues with small hive beetles.

21. Place a **barrier between any colony and any human traffic area** or any animal that is penned or tethered within forty feet. The barrier should be of sufficient density to establish bee flyways above head height.

22. **Maintain a water source** accessible to your colonies located at least half the distance closer than any water source on property owned by others.

23. **Do not open feed.** It encourages robbing, feeds feral bees and those of neighboring beekeepers, may lead to contamination of honey crops and pest and disease transmission among colonies and apiaries.

24. **Avoid opening or disturbing colonies** when neighbors or the general public are participating in outside activities or using machinery within 150 feet of the apiary.

25. **Do not tolerate colonies** exhibiting excessive defensive behavior. Such colonies should be re-queened and the drone brood destroyed.

26. Healthy colonies are valuable and **theft in some areas** could be a problem. Consider **colony placement out of sight** of the general public.

27. **Be a good neighbor** by informing adjoining property owners of the placement of your hives. Address any concerns they may have.

28. Finally, and perhaps most importantly, **keep learning.** Become engaged with the beekeeping community. Maintain a membership with MSBA. Join local beekeeping organizations, we have about four dozen that meet regularly in the Show-Me state. *Learn from others and when you can, give back.* Mentor others in beekeeping.

COACHES AND TEACHERS

One of the hardest concepts for some beginning beekeepers to understand is that they are basically not in charge. They need to learn how to **"read the bees."** They can try to dictate what they want bees to do all they want; that's a lot of work with usually bad consequences for the beekeeper.

If beginning beekeepers can learn how honey bees manage their colonies, it is much easier for the beekeeper to successfully keep bees. In our club we say more experienced beekeepers may be "coaches" but **bees are the "teachers."**

HOW TO STAY UP ON CURRENT INFORMATION

There is also no substitute for keeping up with the latest scientific and research developments with and **about honey bees. Beekeepers re-entering beekeeping** in the last 20 years will find the field **vastly different** from when they started.

Staying on top of scientific developments in the beekeeping community is now a prerequisite for successful beekeeping.

HELPFUL PARTNERS

Before you start feeling overwhelmed, **you have partners** not only in your state beekeeping associations but the state chapters of the National Council of Nonprofits. Many of those groups are charitable nonprofits themselves with the goal of helping others.

For example, our Missouri State Beekeepers Association also helps beekeepers in several ways including:

- Hosting twice a year conferences that bring in leading beekeeping research **scientists to share new information.** It's hard for small local clubs to plan, afford and host some of these speakers.
- Conference breakout sessions featuring local Missouri speakers focused on topics of interest and **customized to local conditions.**
- **Curating resources** so that you know you are referencing reliable information.
- A bi-monthly newsletter provides **new beekeeping information** and upcoming events.

Another benefit of being a member of a state beekeeping association is that by attending conferences you can **tap other beekeepers** about how they run their bee clubs.

- **Plan an initial get-together at a conference** with your neighboring beekeepers to explore their interest in working together to have a bee club. You can focus on getting to know beekeepers from your area while the association does the heavy lifting organizing the meeting.
- You will find a **helpful list** of state and local associations here: American Bee Journal **https://bit.ly/ABJ-Links**
- Bee Culture Magazine **https://www.beeculture.com/find-local-beekeeper**
- If you don't have best management practices for your state, suggest that your state association **develop them.**

OTHER INFORMATION SOURCES

You can also catch the latest scientific beekeeping information at **regional and national beekeeping conferences.** Start by joining and sharing their newsletters and make one of your long-term goals to attend conferences and share information back with your club.

VISIT OTHER BEE CLUBS

I am a big advocate of not re-inventing the wheel so before you plunge into anything, **visit other existing bee clubs** and see how they operate. Observe what **seems to work for them** and what **you think could be improved** for your purposes.

Take that opportunity to meet with the bee club's leadership prior to the meeting and **ask them for advice;** what they would recommend, what pitfalls they navigated through and what suggestions they may have. There is no point in trying to start something from scratch when others have successfully tackled some of the issues, is there?

WHAT IF YOU ARE A BUSINESS WANTING TO SPONSOR A BEE CLUB

Most bee clubs are **charitable educational nonprofits.** Nonprofits can make money for the benefit of the club but not to personally benefit club officers. That's the opposite of the goal of a business, which is profit-motivated.

If you are a business wanting to sponsor a bee club:

1. **Keep your business and bee club activities separate.** Keep separate books, separate bank accounts, separate management. That way there is no question about the club focus being on the success of the beekeepers and the business focus being on the success of your sales.

2. Most people engage with a club expecting it to be a charitable nonprofit educational venture, which means the individuals running the club do not financially benefit. If you mix the two, people may distrust recommendations

and question the motives behind suggestions. **Make it clear** how the business is engaged with the club but don't let the business drive the club.

3. If you want to financially help through the donation of money and items, **make the donation without any strings attached** and make it an outright donation.

4. You will not get a taxable deduction until the club formally incorporates.

5. **Visit other businesses** that sponsor clubs and see how they are operating. If they are in it to make money, they may not be as willing to share information with you, especially if you are in a similar business.

6. Some commercial businesses in major metropolitan areas run **"for profit" bee clubs** where members pay the business to manage their colonies such as "Adopt A Bee Clubs." These "bee clubs" are more service-oriented than educational and information-sharing because members are paying for something to be done. Those bee clubs are set up as part of a commercial business structure and have to abide by **all commercial business tax-collecting and income reporting** requirements. You bet they also have to check with a certified public accountant on how to do that correctly.

YOUR BEST FRIEND IS A CPA

Even before you formally get organized, your best friend will be **a certified public accountant.** They can help guide you in how to best set up your books, track your money and have the basics covered.

If you don't have a CPA as a volunteer, consult with one to identify your best practices and start out on the right foot.

AND GET A BEST FRIEND LAWYER, TOO

In addition to getting your accounting set up properly, tap someone for legal advice and review as well.

States have different legal requirements. Samples in this book are starting points; get someone in your state to review and finalize.

Your Notes

_____

_____

_____

_____

_____

_____

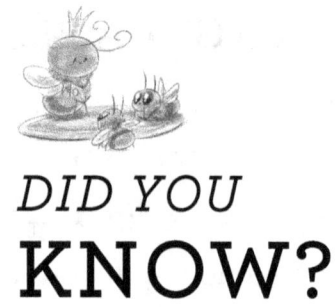

DID YOU KNOW?

- The practice of beekeeping dates back to more than 4,500 years ago.
- In ancient Egypt, people paid their taxes with honey.
- The Magna Carta (1215 AD) legalized the harvesting of wild honey by common folk.

(Courtesy of Beepods.com)

CHAPTER 2

Basic Bee Club Structures

"One can no more approach people without love than one can approach bees without care."

— *Leo Tolstoy, (1828-1910) Russian author and beekeeper*

When I hear the term "bee club" I can easily imagine a bunch of honey bees getting together for a cup of coffee, which inspired this book cover illustration. The fundamental reality of beekeeping is that we as **humans are entering their world.** It is up to us to understand the whys of what they do, not to impose our expectations on them. Those who think the bees do what someone wants, or better yet wait on them, are bound to fail.

In addition, no **two years of beekeeping are the same.** Beekeepers have to juggle a number of factors including local weather, climate, soil, wind, forage and colony conditions among other things. Just as a honey bee colony is dependent on all of its members to do their jobs to be successful, so is a community of beekeepers.

And let's be quite clear. There is something reassuring about listening to other beekeepers' struggles and mistakes as well as successes. **We learn from our mistakes.** It binds us because at one point or another we have all made those mistakes. The struggles and mistakes make the best stories. In the end, a good

Sign in sheets will help you keep track of who is interested in your club and gets you a potential list of volunteers. Write in your full information on the first line – name, address, email, phone number and take your time so it's legible - or the rest of the sign-ins won't fill out all of the lines. Trust me, it helps!

laugh can easily level the playing field, making us all partners in this challenging beekeeping adventure.

HOW TO DEFINE SUCCESS

If there are basic purposes for a bee club, it is **supporting and coaching.** You can read all of the books and watch a ton of videos but beekeeping doesn't become real until you pop that lid and hundreds – well, actually thousands - of honey bees fly into your face.

As I tell our beekeeping students, honey bees don't read books or watch the videos. In the end, **how well each club member keeps honey bees** should be your club's goal and measure of success.

YOUR FIRST MEETINGS

To determine the level of interest in setting up a bee club, it is helpful to **have a couple of meetings** so that you can find others who may be interested in helping. Start with people you know, maybe a fellow beekeeper or someone you see selling honey at a local farmer's market. There may be a science teacher who keeps bees on the side or a garden club with beekeepers. You will need:

- Someone to find **a location** with good parking;
- Make sure there's a **coffee pot** or that one is allowed;
- Set **up a date**;
- **Notify** interested parties;
- **Arrange room** layout and seating.
- If you are meeting online, you will need to **be comfortable** using the platform and set a date and notify interested parties.
- For both meeting options you will need to **plan a program** and **agenda.**

Hold on there, no need to panic about the program, you can **keep the program simple.**

- Ask people attending if they want to start a bee club, what they expect from a club and, maybe the most important question, **what are they willing to contribute** to make one possible.

- At this first meeting, also **discuss the best time** for a follow-up meeting and review who has agreed to do what duties. It may at first feel like you are herding cats but the idea is to make it clear from the beginning **this is a collaborative effort,** not something one person will be expected to do.
- Remember to have a **sign-up sheet** to collect names, addresses, emails and phone numbers so someone can follow-up directly with attendees. If you are meeting online, ask attendees to email their contact information to someone. Note: fully fill in the first line with all information or others will tend not to fill in the spaces. Really!

Sample Sign-Up Sheet

Thanks for signing up to get information about a possible local bee club. Your email will only be used to send meeting and other pertinent bee club information. For more details, contact (Name, phone number, email)

	NAME	ADDRESS	PHONE NUMBER	EMAIL
1.	B. Queen	100 Hive Drive, Bee Town	555-333-8889	4queen@bmail.com
2.				
3.				

PLANNING SECOND MEETING

You have a first good meeting, a second one is in the works. **Now what?**

ESTABLISH AND UNDERSTAND EXPECTATIONS

One of the expectations of a bee club is to get information and guidance about how to successfully keep bees. Since no two years of beekeeping are the same, you want to **"try out"** ways to get that information to share.

- For your second or third organizational meeting, **invite someone local to talk about** what is happening with their bees. Not only will this be helpful but it will give the rest of the group an idea of how a regular club meeting with a speaker might be.
- If there is a nearby club, **tap one of their members** to be a guest speaker.
- If having a guest speaker doesn't seem to work – or even if you have a speaker – try a **round robin beekeeping discussion** asking people attending how their bees are doing. It's interesting to hear what is happening in area apiaries. Sometimes the best meetings are all about listening.

The bottom line is, whatever you do, keep the focus on being **helpful and fun.**

EMPLOYER IDENTIFICATION NUMBER

Once you decide you want to get a bee club established, **there are some basics that are helpful to pursue from the start.**

- Your first piece of business setting up a bee club will be to get an Internal Revenue Service **employer identification number.** This will be the identification number that will identify your club in tax documents, payments and related correspondence.
- You can apply for it **easily online:** https://bit.ly/IRS-Employer-ID

You can also wait to apply for this later but after going through this a few times, I have found getting it early helps to establish a written record and reduces some of the later paperwork.

POSSIBLE BEE CLUB ORGANIZATIONAL STRUCTURES

There are a number of ways you can organize your bee club, ranging from having a minimum of three club officers to four officers and a board of directors. The structure will depend on **what you are trying to accomplish.**

The hardest thing you will do is come up with Bylaws so as you are starting, **don't.** I repeat, **do NOT** start by trying to come up with Bylaws. That's a process for later on when you've **established yourselves** and frankly is not necessary as you start.

Instead, use something like a **sample club charter** to get everyone used to working together until enough funds are raised to formally organize. It will also give everyone **time to sort out** how best they want to run the club and how much work they want to invest in that structure. In most cases, beekeepers want to spend their time talking about bees, not club rules. Right?

BEE CLUB CHARTER

If you think of the principle that you have to **crawl before you walk**, that's the idea behind **a bee club charter**. A charter is basically the reason for having a club and how you plan to operate. It's the **precursor to Bylaws and Articles of Incorporation.**

- **Bylaws** are **internal documents** that outline how the company should be run.
- **Articles of Incorporation are the official documents** you may **file with your state** to start a new club.
  When officially filing for a new club, you usually **include both Articles of Incorporation and Bylaws.** Each state has its own process so check with an attorney or certified public accountant so you understand the process you will have to follow.

It can take a group several years before they are ready to formally start a club so the club charter becomes the guide for how the club **plans to do business.**

- The club charter also has some basic legal requirements included, such as how the club will **dispose of assets** if they decide to disband.
- The **founding philosophy** is also spelled out, such as the club's intention of operating as an educational nonprofit.

Remember it's easier to **start off on the right foot** and get some good habits established than to be sloppy at first and then try to tighten up how the club does business later.

DON'T SIGN, DON'T PLAY

Even through a club charter may be simple and only one page, it is a **binding document** setting your **bee club's intent.** The club charter should include **signatures of the founders** and how you **plan to conduct business.**

- If someone **doesn't want to sign the club charter, they should not continue** on the bee club governing board, even in an advisory role. The bee club board members should all be **operating in the best interests of the bee club.** Getting into that habit early will pay off as the bee club grows and formally organizes.
- Signing the sample club charter is the **first show of good faith** and set of rules everyone agrees to follow.
- It also demonstrates a **personal commitment** by each one who signs that they are working towards the same goals.

TYPES OF NONPROFITS

Alright, now let's go "shopping." The Internal Revenue Service (IRS) grants nonprofit status. Once you complete and receive your nonprofit IRS designation, then you also have to register within your state. Check with your State Attorney General, Secretary of State and/or Consumer Affairs office to determine the process to register your nonprofit in your state.

The following are **six leading nonprofit types** and how they generally operate:

1. **Charitable organizations 501(c)(3).** This is what most people think of when referring to a nonprofit organization. These kinds of charitable organizations are the most popular type of nonprofits.

    - They are primarily funded through donations and government grants.
    - They are allowed to allocate about 10% of their total operating budget on lobbying.
    - **Donations to these nonprofits are tax-deductible.**

2. **Social welfare and civic league organizations 501(c)(4).** Similar to 501(c)(3) in how they operate, these groups can influence politics.

    - **They can publicly endorse and promote legislation to get support and votes.**
    - You cannot get a tax deduction for making contributions to 501(c)(4) organizations.

3. **Social advocacy groups.** Social advocacy groups are 501(c)(4) nonprofits focused on promoting social or political change. Much like the other nonprofits, they promote a certain cause through education and fundraising.

    - **In general, contributions to social advocacy groups are not tax-deductible.**

4. **Social welfare organizations** work to promote social change through fundraising and public awareness. While a social welfare group can lobby for laws to be passed donations are not tax-deductible. Although they are both considered 501(c)(4) organizations, the **main difference between a social welfare organization and a social advocacy group** is whether they focus on lobbying and political influence as their primary driving force for creating change.

5. **Private charitable foundations.** A private charitable foundation is a privately-owned nonprofit established to address broad issues such as education, medical research, environmental issues, and more. They are the nonprofits established by single wealthy benefactors and businesses. They give money to smaller nonprofits.

    - **The money generated by private charitable foundations are not publicly fundraised.** The individual who created the foundation guides how the funds are contributed and invested. The only stipulation is that the initiatives these private charitable foundations donate to must be other 501(c)(3) charities.
    - A private charitable foundation is a registered nonprofit.
    - Contributions up to a certain amount may be tax deductible.

6. **Corporate giving programs.** Corporate giving programs are how businesses donate to charity on behalf of the organization.

    - A corporate giving program is not a registered nonprofit.
    - Corporate giving is individual donations but on a larger scale. Some programs match individual donations as an incentive and provide what part of the donation may be tax-deductible.

NONPROFITS SAME AS NOT-FOR-PROFIT?

Nonprofits **run like a business and try to earn a profit,** which does not support any single member and have a public benefit. Not-for-profits are considered "recreational organizations" that do not operate with the business goal of earning revenue.

CHECK WITH A LAWYER AND ACCOUNTANT

Whatever you decide to do, **check with an attorney and/or certified public accountant** to make sure you are setting up your bee club properly. It is much **easier to fix something early on** than later when bad habits or inappropriate policies of governance have been set in place.

NOW AN EXERCISE FOR INSPIRATION

Think about **other nonprofits you belong to or have belonged to** in the past.

1. What was their purpose and how did they go about meeting that purpose?
2. What worked well and what could have been improved?
3. Are you still a member? Why or why not?
4. What would it take for you to renew your membership? What would it take to make you leave?

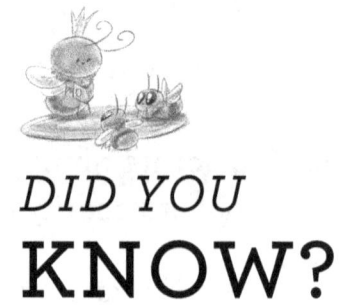

DID YOU **KNOW?**

- The European honey bee was brought over to North America by the Shakers. Because of this, Native Americans referred to honey bees as the "White Man's Fly."
- During the American Revolution, George Washington said "It was the cackling geese that saved Rome, but it was the bees that saved America."
- Honey bees did not spread to Alaska until 1927.

(Courtesy of Beepods.com)

CHAPTER 3

How to Pay Bills

"Like many endeavors, you may want to figure your costs and then double them, just to be on the safe side. I hate to see beekeepers run out of money before they do the things necessary to keep their bees healthy. Caring for bees isn't much different than raising children or pets because unexpected expenses are bound to crop up. Knowing that extra expenses may arise goes a long way to being financially prepared."

*— Rusty Burlew, Beekeeper and author, HoneyBeeSuite.com
and founder Native Bee Conservancy*

Let's face it, the key to having a sustainable bee club, or any club for that matter, is **having enough money** to pay for club necessities: rent, leasing equipment and the all-important coffee so let's review three basic financial club structures. All of these tend to be educational 501(c) 3 nonprofits under Internal Revenue Rules (IRS), which means the clubs can make money to benefit the club but individual club officers cannot financially benefit. More on IRS rules here: **https://bit.ly/IRS-Charitable**

*You never know who may be willing **to share their hive products** to raise club funds. From homemade hives to soaps and other products, welcome donations from, and about, bees. These lovely donated soaps made me wish I wasn't doing the club drawings for that meeting, which disqualifies me. I would have loved to have won those!*

THREE POTENTIAL FINANCIAL STRUCTURES

First, nonprofit does not mean you can't make money. You can. It's **who benefits** from those funds that's the issue. As a nonprofit, **all proceeds benefit only the club,** not individual club members and/or board members.

The following are **three possible** nonprofit bee club financial structures:
- Membership with dues.
- Donations.
- Item sales proceeds.

Here's a summary of the **main pros and cons** of each of these bee club structures.

BEE CLUB MEMBERSHIP WITH DUES

Bee clubs with dues-paying membership is the **traditional bee club structure.** There are a number of reporting requirements associated with having dues paying members. If you don't like paperwork and process, this option **will be challenging.** In Missouri, membership-based clubs have yearly reporting requirements and make decisions by majority vote if it's not spelled out in a set of Bylaws.

When joining a membership dues club, ask to see a **copy of the Bylaws** so you know how they plan to operate. The Bylaws are supposed to be how they will be **accountable to you,** the dues-paying member.

If you join a membership bee club and they can't provide a copy of their Bylaws, **leave.** You don't want to be associated with a group that plays by their own unspecified rules or give them money that they can't account for how it is being used.

On the other hand, membership-based bee clubs have an **easier way** of keeping track of area beekeepers and sharing information.

BEE CLUBS FUNDED BY DONATIONS

Donations are the option **favored by new bee clubs** in the last few years. Although some do well asking for money, beginning bee clubs can often come up short of funds. Service clubs, churches and most nonprofits have a minimum they **carry over** from year to year to make sure they can cover their basic operational expenses.

To that end, the first goal of your club should be to come up with an **estimated budget** for operations, then raise funds to cover those costs. A sample bee club beginning expense estimate is at the end of this chapter.

It is helpful to have members who are willing to kick in funds when money is short but unrealistic to expect that to happen indefinitely. The issue with those last-minute contributions is that the rest of the membership may assume someone else will pay for club costs indefinitely. I only recommend **collecting donations** for **start-up funding** with the understanding that, at some point, the club will pay them back and start generating funds some other way.

Make it clear to everyone that **any loan** will be paid back and when. There should be no misunderstanding of who is funding the club and getting repaid.

At some point the bee club should have **other funding sources** to pay for estimated costs.

PROCEEDS FROM SELLING ITEMS

Selling items is the third option to generate funds to cover expenses without having some of the legal responsibilities associated with a membership-based club. To manage finances through item sales, it is helpful to have **someone experienced in running a business** who understands how to buy, price and manage club inventory.

Here are some of the basic principles to do this smoothly:

1. If a business donates items, remember to provide **confirming written documentation** to the donating business.
2. Should you reimburse the donor for the wholesale cost? My accountant said no, keep the **donation clean and one way only**. If you want to donate an item, give it free and clear.
3. Should the bee club buy hats, t-shirts, bags with a club logo? **Choose patches instead.** Then bee club members can sew those on to whatever they want to display their bee club pride and the club isn't trying to carry all of the different sizes, find storage space, haul those items to club meetings. It's a popular item for discussion but not a very practical one, especially for a beginning group.

4. There are other "on demand" services that provide logo-specific products. Do your homework first and **some market research** to see if people are willing to pay the higher prices.
5. **Check with a certified public accountant** on how you are setting up the club's business records to make sure you are following best practices.

ESTIMATE WHAT FUNDS YOU WILL NEED

Can a club use all three funding structures? Yes, as a bee club grows, the organization can move from one to the next and even combine structures. To prepare for these options, you will need **a "guess-timate"** of how much money your bee club may need to operate from year to year. It may take you a year to come up with good figures so keep track of all of your expenses through that year. Why?

People will be more willing to help you if they know **what funds you need** and how you **plan to spend those funds.**

Start with simple financial cost projections that include:

- Room **rental fees**
- **Online meeting platform expenses**
- **Coffee** and refreshments
- **Photocopying costs** (check your local UPS store for their yearly copy sales usually November and March)
- **Equipment costs:** projector/screen/computer purchase/rental

There will be **other expenses** but these will give you a beginning estimated cost figure for the funds you will need to get started.

If you plan to have special events, include projections of those costs since most events don't recapture their costs until after money is needed to pay bills.

OPTIONS FOR GETTING START-UP FUNDS

Well yes, you will need to get some money to get started. Here are some options on **how to get those start-up funds:**

- Some organizations such as chambers of commerce and planning commissions have **grant programs** for club start-ups so check with your community groups. These tend to be one-time awards and require detailed follow-up documentation. Read the guidelines carefully and make sure you can follow them.
- **Local businesses** that carry bee equipment may invest in a bee club since they will benefit from future beekeeping equipment customers. Some companies will only donate once the club has their IRS nonprofit status and the company gets their tax deduction but it doesn't hurt to ask.
- **Big box stores** have community grant programs they award on a regular basis. There is a written application process and a reporting requirement where you show in writing and photos how you spent the awarded funds. Contact them directly for their application process and follow the directions.
- Some **local companies** may have an associated foundation that may provide seed money so check their funding guidelines.
- If you have a beekeeping-related company and want to help by donating equipment and funds, make sure the donations to the bee club are made **without strings attached** or it can backfire on your company. Check first with a CPA to make sure you are following best practices.
- **Ask for donations** from people attending your meetings.
- **Sell donated items** at your meetings.
- **Hold a bake sale** around a time when people can use home baked goods such as holidays: Mother's Day (May), Father's Day (June), Grandparents Day (September), Thanksgiving (November) and Christmas (December) are good months to offer baked items for sale.
- **Buy items to resell** at a higher price such as sugar. The challenge here is you need money to buy the sugar to re-sell and there is a workload associated with getting the sugar to its final destination, placing it in smaller containers, taking orders and

*You may be surprised to find potential club members, and relatives, have amazing baking skills and would be **willing to share them for the cause.***

collecting money. Make sure you have someone keeping track of the sugar orders who is accountable to someone not involved in the details. Check with an attorney and/or accountant, or better yet an attorney who is an accountant, to make sure you are not responsible for taxes and such.

OPTIONS FOR GETTING OTHER FUNDING

Some states have **partnerships** where groups will work together to apply for grants and cost-share. You will need to be formally-organized to participate in most of these programs.

To apply for grants, make sure to **read and follow grant requirements to the letter.** Some grant reviews will kick out applicants if they don't follow the format, order of requested information and so forth.

Double-check your writing; you want your application free of spelling errors.

Most grants require how you will prove how you used the money so plan on having someone **document your activities** with photos, flyers and other examples so you can include those in your final report.

If you've never applied for a grant, **find examples from past years.** Most grants will have a list of winning applicants and their proposals on their websites.

if you are close to an Extension office, **check if they have someone** who can help you write the grant.

SO HOW MUCH DOES A CLUB NEED FOR A YEAR?

Keep track of your expenses with receipts so you have an accurate accounting.

Here's a **sample estimate of bee club costs** and its associated expenses including both in person meetings and using online platforms. These days we need to plan for both.

Look at **other clubs** and note what they are doing and how much it costs them.

Start simple and build from there; **don't over-extend yourself.**

Focus first on the basics for the meetings; then slowly add **program and associated expense.**

SAMPLE BEE CLUB EXPENSES ESTIMATE

EXPENSE	AMOUNT	THIS YEAR	NEXT YEAR	NOTES
Monthly Rent and Online Meeting Platform cost	$25* $15	(11 months) $275* $150	(11 months)	*possible rent increase next year
Coffee/Tea/Water Treats	$15	$165		
Business cards Chair rental	$25 $20	$25 $220		
Projector rental Computer rental	$10 $10	$110 $110		
Postage	$10	$110		
Name Tags	$5	$55		
Copies	$50	$50 One time		
Honey Tasting Awards	$25	$25		
Door Prizes	$50	$50		
Bee Club Basics Book, 2nd Edition bluebirdgardens.com/books	$34.95	(5 copies) $174.75		One for each officer and one to loan out
Subtotal GOAL for Next Year	-------	$1,410	$1,500	

Your Notes

_____

_____

_____

_____

_____

_____

_____

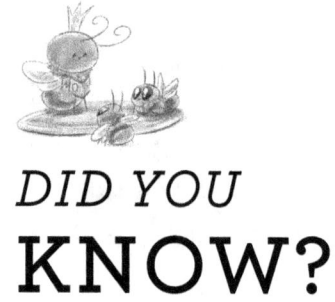

DID YOU KNOW?

- The first Anglo-Saxons drank beer made from water and honeycomb, with herbs for flavoring.
- Mead, which is made from fermented honey, is the world's oldest fermented beverage.
- Honey bees are attracted to caffeine.

(Courtesy of Beepods.com)

CHAPTER 4

Organizing a Bee Club

"In the long history of humankind (and animal kind too) those who learned to collaborate and improvise most effectively have prevailed."
— *Charles Darwin, (1809-1882) British biologist and beekeeper*

Your first exploratory meetings have gone well, you have reviewed your possible bee club structures and funding options, and now **you are ready to get a club started. Congratulations, that's an exciting place to be!**

To get a bee club organized, start with a **planning group of 3-5 volunteers** who are willing to devote time to the effort. You may already have a group of friends who enjoy talking bees so **tap them** about helping to pull a more formal group together. Be forewarned, however, that a group of beekeepers who are friends may be more interested in talking bees than how to organize a club. **Make it clear** why you are getting together, and **allow time for some bee talk** but don't let them guide you too far off track. You are there to talk about getting a bee club organized. Goals, remember?

*Honey bees are not the only ones attracted to coffee, so are some beekeepers. The secret to a good "in person" meeting is to **have the coffee ready** and waiting, and compost the coffee grounds. They are excellent rose food!*

STARTING FROM SCRATCH

- **Call people who have successful clubs** for advice and invite them to meet. They don't have to be bee clubs; most educational nonprofits operate on the same principles.
- **Visit other clubs** either in person and/or online. Observe what they do; follow up with questions.
- **Check with your state association of nonprofits** for advice and assistance.
- **Plan a couple of exploratory meetings.** Brainstorm what yours goals may be and what you think you can accomplish.
- Know that some beekeepers don't want to be involved in running a club so some **start up advisors may not be beekeepers.**

RE-INVIGORATING AN EXISTING CLUB?

- **Do a little homework.** What was working well in the past? What needs improvement?
- **Tap club founders** for help to get club back on track.
- **Review and revise** your purpose and goals, maybe those need to be adjusted and/or changed.
- **Ask beekeepers.** What do they want from their club?
- **Be patient.** It may take a little time for former members to return.

BEE CLUB PLANNING TEAM

The initial bee club planning team will be important but not necessarily vital to the club's success. Include someone on the planning group **that runs another club** so you can tap into expertise as well as challenges.

- The bee club planning team will need to devote some time to getting the club off the ground and established, or re-invigorated. Make sure your planning team is comprised of **people who like and trust each other.**
- Once the planning team agrees on the bee club goals and how they plan to operate, **put it in writing** and have everyone sign and date it. You will find a suggested **charter agreement** at the end of this chapter. A lawyer

drew up and recommended this agreement but please double check with your own counsel since laws can be different. The most important part of the signed charter agreement is how any **collected assets** – from money to physical equipment – will be disposed of in the event the bee club closes. States may vary on those requirements.

Spend the first couple of planning team organizational meetings talking about **why you want to meet** and **ask for volunteers to help.**

- **Do NOT assume all of the work on yourself**, or assume someone else will do it all. Find someone you can trust to get it done and who is willing to take it on. You may need to work with a number of people before you can find reliable volunteers. Make sure they **have back up** so that someone can fill in for each other.
- Usually at these first organizational meetings, time is devoted to coming up with a **bee club name.** That's fine, it's a good exercise to bring the group together but it is not necessary, that can come later. When in doubt, keep the name simple and name the club after the place where you will meet. That makes identification easier!
- The planning team will be operating as your **executive committee**, usually comprised of a president, vice-president, secretary, treasurer and a past president. The executive committee is usually the group that manages the day to day club operations.

ESTABLISH CLEAR EXPECTATIONS FROM THE START

From the outset, make it clear:

- **Everyone will have to pitch in** with time and money. Don't let a rental bill for a meeting room or an online platform build up past the second organizational meeting without making attendees accountable. Rotate who pays for the room, take up a collection or otherwise address it up front and directly.
- **Plan to collect emails** so you have a mailing list for follow up contacts.
- If you are comfortable with social media, set up a **Facebook group page** after you have a name. Closed Facebook groups are a good option if you

are just starting and want some time to settle into your meeting routine. It's also a safer and more comfortable forum for people to post questions.

- Note: if you want a **Facebook nonprofit page so you can accept donations,** you need to have all of your legal documents set up. You can't change another page into a nonprofit page.

ASSESS VOLUNTEER INTEREST

After the first couple of organizational meetings, convene the planning team and assess interest and **who is willing to help.** Be honest and compare who is interested against your goals. Frankly if no one steps up, keep getting together over coffee and at state and regional conferences. **Let some momentum build** before you tackle setting up, or restarting, a bee club.

If you have a good group of volunteers, **follow up with their tasks** for the next meeting:

- **Call them** to make sure they are on board, understand what they are doing and where.
- **Follow-up emails** with reminders.
- If people are nervous about how you plan to meet, **have a practice session.**
    - Try out different **chair arrangements.**
    - **Walk through** where you want to set up the coffee pot.
    - **Identify** bathroom locations and emergency exits.
    - Check for **internet service.**
    - Double check **who has the room key**!
- Online meetings will also go smoother if you **have a dry run.**

WHERE TO MEET

Check city hall, courthouses, local schools and churches for potential public meeting rooms with good access. Make sure:

- **Meeting rooms are easy to reach. Do they** have stairs and/or an elevator.

- **Is there ample parking?**
- **Tobacco use policy**; is/is not allowed.
- **The place is easy to find with GPS.** Yes, double check the address on your cell phone map application(s) to make sure they will guide people to the correct location. Once my cell phone assistant misunderstood a club meeting address and tried to insist that I was heading to the Cayman Islands. Don't I wish!
- **Find out building rules:**
  - When does the building open and close.
  - Can you bring in your own food.
  - Is there enough space to socially distance (usually 6 feet apart)
  - Are firearms allowed.
  - Point of contact for issues.

NO SUCH THING AS FREE MEETING SPACE

The days of "free" space are gone so know that at some point **you will need to pay** for a meeting room, either by paying a monthly rental/leasing fee or through a yearly "donation." **Even churches** these days are now trying to recover overhead expenses so if meeting in a church, budget for a year end "donation" to thank them for their space. A good rule of thumb is $300.

Be aware that some people have issues meeting at a religious location:
- Explain that this is the **only known available location.**
- **Solicit help** finding a better meeting location alternative.
- Most churches don't get involved with meetings in their community rooms.
- Don't underestimate the influence of **supplying an organization with local honey** in exchange for a meeting room!

DEVELOP LIST OF POTENTIAL MEETING SITES

Keep a list of all potential sites in case one is not available on your regular meeting date. You don't want to have to go searching again if you need another site.

If you can find a **location close to an apiary** that can be accessed around club meeting dates that can be helpful later on.

SAMPLE MEETING ROOM COMPARISON CHECK LIST						
NAME ADDRESS	RENT COST	PARKING	COFFEE POT	TOBACCO FREE	HANDICAP ACCESS	OTHER (HOURS)

YOUR FIRST PURCHASE, A COFFEE POT!

If there is one symbol of getting together it's the coffee pot so this may turn out to be **your first official purchase.** Some meeting rooms **come equipped** with coffee pots but if not:

- **Borrow a coffee pot** until you know how many people may be attending your meetings. Return the pot with some coffee as a thanks for the loan.
- **Be open to someone donating** your first coffee pot.
- **Shop local thrift shops.** Pick up one coffee pot for coffee and the second to heat water for tea and hot cocoa. If you don't know what to get, pick up a small coffee pot that can be later used for heating water, then gauge what larger size coffee pot you may need.
- **Try local dollar stores** for paper cups and plates, and keep a running tally to get reimbursed.
- **Have one person** responsible for the coffee pot and associated items.
- **Start delegating early** so that meeting responsibilities don't all fall on one person.
- Encourage a **donation of honey** for your coffee station.

MATCH MEETING ROOM LAYOUT WITH MEETING OBJECTIVES

Once you have a room, **consider the layout.** If you have a small group, start with **chairs in a U-shape** so that everyone feels included. Once the meetings have programs and other activities, move the chairs and tables around to make the room better accessible for the planned activity.

Ensure that whatever layout you use, it **allows for people to see as well as hear** what is happening.

COVID-RELATED MEETING ISSUES

Until the current pandemic is over, include **COVID-related** meeting considerations:

- Meet in a large area that allows **for social distancing** (usually at least 6 feet apart)
- Keep chairs **at least 6 feet apart.**
- **Encourage mask-wearing** for everyone.
- Add **soap and hand sanitizer** to sign-in areas, coffee areas and bathrooms.
- **Do not share open food items.**

BEE CLUB SOCIAL HOUR

Regardless of how informal or formal your bee club meetings are, **plan for a social hour** before the actual meeting.

- A social hour will allow **shy and introverted people to discuss their issues** without having to bring them up in front of the whole group.
- This informal gathering opportunity will also help attendees to **better get to know each other** and share stories.

If you are meeting online, **develop a list of questions** to prompt informal discussion. Send people a PDF document with "agree" and "disagree" so they can print those words off and easily participate in answering. Remember, keep **making it fun!**

BEE CLUB REFRESHMENTS

The bee club should be able to offer coffee, tea and water as a minimum. **Set out donation cans** and ask people to pay if they help themselves to refreshments.

- When meeting in person, and before the pandemic, we also offered **foods that were pollinated by bees**: nuts, vegetables, fruits, seeds and berries.
- We also encouraged people to bring snacks **made with honey.**

It's another opportunity to **educate attendees** about the role honey bees play in our food chain.

STAY ON TIME!

Such a simple concept but one so easily forgotten, and can leave you wondering why no one shows up for your next meeting.

- **Start your meetings on time;** stick to the time schedule and plan for a 10 to 15-minute break at the 50-minute mark.
- If you have something at the last minute you want to offer later, do so and make it clear **it's optional.** Sharing whatever the activity is beforehand will significantly improve your chances of having participants so sparingly spring last minute special activities.

- Share your meeting agenda **at least one week prior** to the meeting. That will give people a chance to review the items and come prepared for planned discussions and activities.

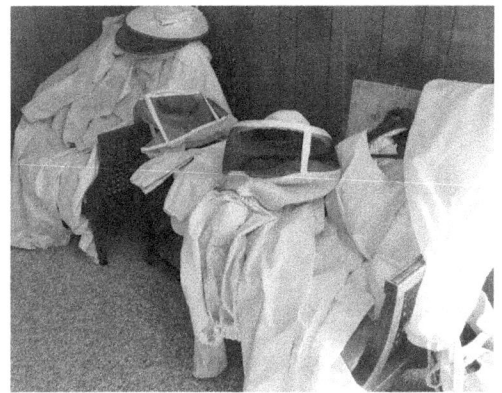

*One of the services we provide during our classes and club meetings is to bring in examples of basic beekeeping equipment. That helps beginning beekeepers better understand what the items are and **encourages them to ask questions.***

BASIC BEEKEEPING HELP

Overwhelmed? It can feel that way so let's get back to why you are meeting and how to make that **not only fun but helpful.** I know, you want a speaker but that's not a deal breaker, you have plenty of opportunities to be helpful with whoever is attending your meetings.

When our club started, one of the services we provided was bringing in our bee suits. Some had full suits, others had jackets and pith helmets with veils. And gloves, bee glove sizes vary widely. We did wash the suits – or I did at least – so that new beekeepers could try them on. This fashion show of sorts was also included in my beginning beekeeping classes, either as part of the class and/or available during class breaks. You can spend **a good meeting discussing:**

- Pros and cons of bee suits and gloves, and how to wash bee suits and gloves.
- 8-frame versus 10-frame hives. Weight when filled with honey; strength of beekeeper's back.
- Various hive tools and how each is used and why.
- Telescoping versus garden hive covers.

In other words, **bring things in that will prompt a good conversation.**

BEE CLUB MEETING GIVEAWAYS

Here's another way to get a good conversation going. Who doesn't like to get something for free? Giving items away is a **good educational opportunity.**

- Don't just hand over items, **provide an explanation** of how to use each of the items as you give them away.
- Better yet, **ask someone in the group to do so** to encourage participation. That way the event becomes educational as well as motivational, and others in the bee club who did not get the item benefit as well.

At the Rolla Bee Club, we use the sign-up sheet as people come in and number the names, rotating what number we start with every month. Then another person selects numbers without seeing the list. **Club coaches managing the giveaways are not included** in the drawing list so that there is no question about who was selected.

You can **get giveaways** by:

- **Asking companies** you regularly buy from.
- **Asking vendors** at conferences.
- **Welcoming other beekeepers** who may be willing to share.
- **Direct item purchases**.

Remember to **recognize and thank** whoever donated items.

Check with the businesses that provided items as well, they may **want a receipt** for taxes and their records.

Be **wary of clubs that wield giveaways** to entice people to attend meetings. If the only reason someone is attending your club meetings is to get free items, you need to **seriously rethink** what you are doing. It can happen periodically but you want your regular members to benefit from the giveaways so monitor who is getting the free items and make adjustments accordingly.

BEE CLUB MEETING "SHOW AND TELL"

It's the easiest thing to do, sit around and just talk about bees. But if you are starting, you don't know the difference between a super and an "Illinois." (If you're just starting, those are the very same thing.)

Print photos of basic beekeeping functions – this is a swarm cell on a frame – on 8.5x11 inch card stock for easy handling as it gets passed around. I keep a supply of these kinds of basic photos in a portable file so they can be accessed when we are doing a presentation or, better yet, answering questions.

As you plan your meetings, **think about what else you can take to club meetings** to demonstrate what you are going to discuss at that meeting. One of my favorite "show and tell" examples was a frame of dead bees my bee buddy David saved from a colony that had died over winter. He carefully wrapped and stored it in the freezer until our club meeting time, then brought it to the meeting early. By the time the meeting started, that frame had filled our meeting room with an unmistakable aroma people are still talking about today.

- David had the right idea, **bring in samples** of what you see in a hive.
- Also **share photos and videos** of what you are observing. Sometimes the main activity during our social hour – besides drinking coffee – is sharing still photos and recordings on cell phones. It's a great way to get more accurate advice than to try to describe what you are seeing in your hives, especially if you are a new beekeeper.
- If you have equipment to include **slide and video presentations** in your meetings, even better but that's usually a goal for beginning clubs. Even after all of these years of being organized and having slide presentations, our bee club still enjoys the **hands-on aspect** of seeing actual beekeeping tools and beekeeping-related photos.

BEE CLUB MEETING CLEAN UP

Before ending the meeting, ask volunteers to help with the bee club meeting tear down and clean up. It may take longer to supervise people doing it than one person doing it all but this is **another opportunity** to build community. People will usually help if they know what needs to be done.

Remember to **thank them for helping.** If we are safely able to share donated food, share meeting leftovers for them to take home.

AFTER MEETING APIARY VISITS

If you are meeting close to an apiary, that's a good opportunity to introduce people to bees and experience seeing the world through a bee suit. If your club **doesn't have insurance** yet, **don't sponsor the visit.** Let the apiary owner invite people to see his/her apiary.

Some **tips on planning an apiary visit**:

- **Establish a time** for the proposed apiary visit, weather permitting, and **provide advance notice** of the visit so attendees can prepare.
- Insist that **all wear protective gear;** a bee jacket or jumpsuit and gloves.
- Provide a little **safety talk** before heading to the hives.
- If using a **smoker, assign someone** to tend to the smoker at all times.
- Have **First Aid on hand** including an EpiPen®.
- Warn everyone **not to walk on the flowers**!

AFTER BEE CLUB MEETING REVIEW

Plan to spend a few minutes after every meeting **going over what went well**, what needs to be addressed and improved, and what you want to do at your next meeting. It's much easier to do it **immediately following the** current meeting than to try to remember it later.

And **create an open environment** where people can make suggestions to change and improve meetings. Circumstances change; volunteers leave. Practice making regular meeting adjustments and your team will have another opportunity to learn how to work together.

Someone defensive? Let them have their say; then follow-up with a private conversation about why you have these discussions and how they are not personal but done in the club's best interests.

Your Notes

Your Notes

_____

_____

_____

_____

_____

_____

_____

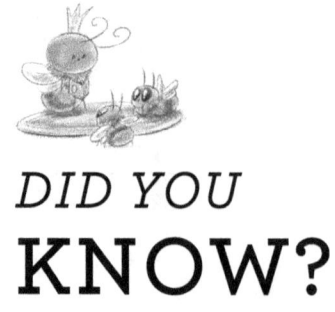

DID YOU KNOW?

- In Greek mythology, Apollo is credited as being the first beekeeper.
- The ancient Greeks minted coins with bees on them.
- The name 'Melissa' is derived from the Greek word for honey bee.

(Courtesy of Beepods.com)

CHAPTER 5

Getting "Paperwork" Organized

"It takes as much energy to wish as it does to plan."
— Eleanor Roosevelt
Wife of U.S. President Franklin D. Roosevelt from 1933-1945

There are several ways an educational nonprofit bee club can get "paperwork organized." From getting business cards to developing a Charter, then Bylaws and Articles of Incorporation, these are the key steps to becoming a formal club.

BUSINESS CARDS

Get business cards made and distributed to your planning team members so they can pass them out with pertinent information; name of club, meeting location, contact phone numbers. If you design these with a blank spot to write in an upcoming meeting date, you can all use them throughout the year.

Business cards can be as simple as one sided with basic information in black and white or two-sided, in color cards. These were designed and printed by Vista Print. Our club planning team members carry these and hand them out when they meet someone who is interested in beekeeping.

*Once you settle on a meeting format, **give it a try** for a year and see how it works for everyone. People like to have a consistent meeting format so they know what to expect when. Except for December. Then plan something festive and fun – ho ho ho!*

CLUB CHARTER AGREEMENT

Develop a **Club Charter agreement,** which is a basic set of Bylaws. Use the Club Charter agreement until you know how you want to operate and have the funding to officially organize.

- **Check with your secretary of state's office** or state attorney general on how soon you need to have Bylaws. Most states allow for several years before those are required.
- Try out different ways to operate until you find the format that is comfortable for your planning team and volunteers.

Bylaws are a more **detailed explanation** of the Club Charter agreement. By using a Club Charter and having a history of how you want to run your club, you will have a majority of the answers you will need for when you develop Bylaws.

SAMPLE BEGINNING CLUB CHARTER AGREEMENT

ARTICLE 1: NAME AND PURPOSE

Section 1: The name of the organization shall be Sample Bee Club at Sample.com.

Section 2: Sample Bee Club was formed to increase public awareness of beekeeping; to support nonpartisan research and to educate beekeepers about beekeeping.

ARTICLE II: MEMBERSHIP

Section 3: No dues. There may be fees associated with classes and special events; the club will be run as a nonprofit corporation under its own employer identification number associated with (any sponsoring organizations)

Section 4: The Executive Committee shall have the authority to establish and define membership categories, class fees and any other fees associated with club management.

ARTICLE III: MEETINGS OF MEMBERS

Section 5: Monthly meetings shall be held at (day of month, time, address.) One or more of the Executive Board members will preside over the meetings.

Section 6: Special meetings may be called by any one of the Executive Board members.

ARTICLE IV: EXECUTIVE BOARD

Section 7: The Executive Board is responsible for overall policy and club direction.

Section 8: The Executive Board shall meet at least quarterly, at an agreed upon time and place, to plan the club's upcoming activities.

Section 9: There shall be three members of the Executive Board. The board will keep records, including overseeing the taking of minutes at meetings and assuring that corporate records are maintained. The board will work on training schedules for club meetings and meeting logistical support. Duties may be moved around board members at the board's discretion.

Section 10: One person shall make financial information available to the board.

Section 11: In the event the Executive Board disbands, the Executive Board members will dispose of all club equipment and assets in such a manner as not to benefit themselves individually but benefit other similar nonprofits.

ARTICLE V: AMENDMENTS

These charter bylaws may be amended by a majority of the Executive Board.

Approved: (Date) and signed by Executive Board members.

Now don't just copy and fill in your bee club name, you need to make sure this simple kind of document complies with your state laws. **Check with an attorney** on the easiest way to get started.

BEE CLUB NONPROFIT ARTICLES OF INCORPORATION

Most states require Articles of Incorporation and Bylaws so they know how you plan to operate.

Make sure you **understand the legal meaning** and purpose behind your Bylaws and Articles of Incorporation. Do not just "use" another club's Bylaws.

This is a simple sample Articles of Incorporation developed by a lawyer. I would also suggest **consulting a lawyer** once you have your proposed structure to **make sure it meets your state requirements.** (Humm, where have you heard that before?)

SAMPLE BEE CLUB NONPROFIT ARTICLES OF INCORPORATION

The undersigned natural person(s) of the age of eighteen years of age for the purpose of forming a corporation under the Missouri Nonprofit Corporation Law adopt the following Articles of Incorporation:

1. The name of the corporation is Sample Bee Club, Inc.
2. The corporation is a Public Benefit Corporation.

3. The period of duration of the corporation is perpetual. The name and street address of the Registered Agent and the Registered Office is Sample Club Organizer, Sample Lane, Sample, MO. 00000. (The registered agent or statutory agent should be the current treasurer. Ensure this agent is updated as needed. The club should also determine if it wants to use a post office box for the main address so that mail doesn't end up lost at a personal address as officers change.)

4. The name and address of the incorporator is Sample, 000 Sample Lane, Sample, Mo. 00000.

5. The corporation shall not have any members.

6. The corporation is formed for the following purposes:

    a. The corporation is organized exclusively for charitable, religious, educational and scientific purposes, including, for such purposes, the making of distributions to organizations that qualify as exempt organizations under section 501(c)(3) of the Internal Revenue Code, or the corresponding section of any future federal tax code.

    b. By way of qualification, it is hereby further provided that:
    (1) No part of the net earnings of the corporation shall inure to the benefit of, or be distributable to is members, trustees, officers or other private persons, except that the corporation shall be authorized and empowered to pay reasonable compensation for services rendered and to make payments and distributions in furtherance of the purposes set forth herein.
    (2) No substantial part of the activities of the corporation shall be the carrying on of propaganda, or otherwise attempting to influence legislation, and the corporation shall not participate in, or intervene in (including the publishing or distribution of statements) any political campaign on behalf of or in opposition to any candidate for public office.

7. Notwithstanding any other provision of these Articles, the corporation shall not carry on any other activities not permitted to be carried on

    a. by a corporation exempt from federal income tax under section 501(c)(3) of the Internal Revenue code, or the corresponding section of any future federal tax code, or

b. by a corporation, contributions to which are deductible under section 170(c)(2) of the Internal Revenue Code, of the corresponding section of any future federal tax code.

8. Upon the dissolution of the corporation, assets shall be distributed for one of more exempt purposes within the meaning of section 501(c)(3) of the Internal Revenue Code, or the corresponding section of any future federal tax code, or shall be distributed to the federal government, or to a state or local government, for a public purpose. Any such assets not so disposed of shall be disposed of by the Circuit Court of (local county, state) or some other Court of competent jurisdiction of the county in which the principal office of the corporation is then located, exclusively for such purposes or to such organization or organizations, as said Court shall determine, which are organized and operated exclusively for such purposes.

   c. To exercise all rights and powers conferred upon it by the provisions of the laws of (your resident state) generally pertaining to nonprofit corporations, including, without limiting the generality of any of the foregoing to acquire by bequest, devise, gift, purchase, lease or otherwise, either absolutely or in trust, any property of any sort or nature without limitation as to its amount of value, and to hold, invest, reinvest, manage, use, apply, employ, sell, expend, disperse, lease, mortgage, convey, donate or otherwise dispose of such property, and the income, principal and proceeds thereof, for any of the purposes herein set forth.

9. The effective date of this document is the date it is filed by the Secretary of State of (your state).

The undersigned swears that the matters set forth in the foregoing petition are true and correct according to their best knowledge, information and belief, subject to the penalties of making a false affidavit or declaration.

IN AFFIRMATION THEREOF, the facts stated above are true and correct according to the best knowledge, information and belief of the undersigned, subject to the penalties provided under (your state statutes)

(Signed by the incorporator)

Remember to check with an attorney to make sure your proposed Articles of Incorporation meet your state requirements.

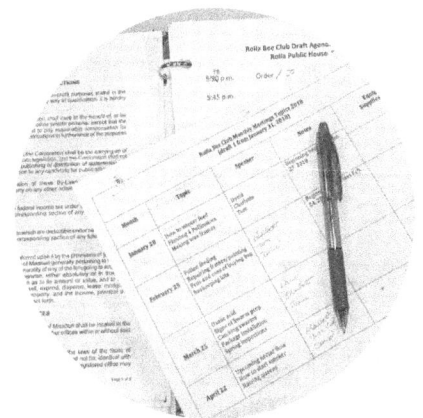

*Keep **both electronic and hard copies** of your club's key documents so they can be easily retrieved. If they have been officially filed, you can usually also get a copy from your secretary of state's office.*

BEE CLUB BYLAWS

The term "Bylaws" has developed a **negative connotation** over the years so use "rules," "how we plan to operate" and "what we're going to do" as options for the same thing: **how you plan to run the bee club**.

To develop these, I suggest the bee club planning team work under first **proposed bee Club Charter rules** to comfortably sort out details. Remember to consult with an attorney so you know your state requirements. Part of the challenge is getting to know what the group can and can't do under certain organizational structures and state requirements so take your time doing the research. Keep whatever you decide to do **clear and simple.** One of hardest things you will do later is change them so try them out for size before going formal.

- You can find sample bee club Bylaws and organizational structures for free online.
- Remember to **update your annual club expenses** to incorporate these additional fees for the year you plan to formally incorporate.
    - For planning purposes, filing for a **nonprofit educational 501(c)(3) club with the IRS** runs around $500.
    - Then there will be **state filing fees** which vary from state to state. Missouri Secretary of State's filing fee is $75.

- If you use online forums, those range from $275 on up depending on how you structure your bee club.
- **Legal review fees vary.** Most lawyers have set fees for various documents. Developing Articles of Incorporation and Bylaws from scratch can range from $400-$2,000.

SAMPLE NONPROFIT BEE CLUB BYLAWS FOR A NONPROFIT CORPORATION

ARTICLE I – PURPOSES AND RESTRICTIONS

The purposes of the Corporation shall be those nonprofit purposes stated in the Articles of Incorporation, as they may be amended. By way of qualification, it is hereby further provided that:

A. No part of the net earnings of the Corporation shall inure to the benefit of, or be distributable to its members, trustees, officers, or other private persons, except that the Corporation shall be authorized and empowered to pay reasonable compensation for services rendered and to make payments and distributions in furtherance of the purposes set forth in the Articles of Incorporation.

B. No substantial part of the Corporation activities shall be the carrying on of propaganda, or otherwise attempting to influence legislation, and the Corporation shall not participate in, or intervene in (including the publishing or distribution of statements) any political campaign on behalf of or in opposition to any candidate for public office.

C. Notwithstanding any other provision of these By-Laws or Articles of Incorporation, the Corporation shall not carry on any other activities not permitted to be carried on:

a. by a corporation exempt from federal income tax under section 501(c)(3) of the Internal Revenue Code, or the corresponding section of any future federal tax code, or

b. by a corporation, contributions to which are deductible under section 170 (c)(2) of the Internal Revenue Code, or the corresponding section of any future federal tax code.

D. To exercise all rights and powers conferred upon it by the provisions of (cite state laws) generally pertaining to nonprofit corporations, including, without limiting the generality of any of the foregoing to acquire by bequest, devise, gift, purchase, lease of otherwise, either absolutely or in trust, any property of any sort or nature without limitation as to is amount of value, and to hold, invest, reinvest, manage, use, apply, employ, sell, expend, disperse, lease, mortgage, convey, donate or otherwise dispose of such property, and the income, principal and proceeds thereof, for any of the purposes herein set forth.

ARTICLE II – OFFICES

The principal office of the Corporation in the (name the state) shall be located in the (name of city). The Corporation may have such other offices within or without said City as may be required.

The registered office of the Corporation required under the laws of the (name state) to be maintained in the (name of state) may be, but not need be, identical with the principal office in the (name of state) and the address of the registered office may be changed from time to time in conformity with the laws of (name of state). The Corporation shall maintain a registered agent whose address shall be the same as that of the registered Corporation office.

ARTICLE III – MEMBERS

The Corporation shall not have shareholders or members.

ARTICLE IV – BOARD OF DIRECTORS

A. **Management.** Corporation affairs shall be managed, supervised and controlled by a self-perpetuating Board of Directors consisting of not less than THREE (3) persons and not more than SEVEN (7) persons elected by a majority of the Board in a manner specified in paragraph B herein below. ONE (1) of the initial directors shall serve a one (1) year term; ONE (1) of the initial directors shall serve a two (2) year term: and ONE (1) of the initial directors shall serve a THREE (3) year term.

B. **Term and Election of Directors.** The full term of office of directors shall be THREE (3) years, and to the extent practicable taking into account increases or decreases in the number of directors constituting the Board of Directors, one-third (1/3) of the Board of Directors shall be elected each year at the annual meeting of the Board of Directors, the directors so elected filing the place of retiring directors. In the event of a change in the number of directors, the resolution effectuating such change shall specify the years in which the terms of the directorships thereby created shall first expire. Vacancies occurring in the Board of Directors, including vacancies due to an increase in the number of directors, may be filled by the directors then in office. Any director may serve an indefinite number of terms.

C. **Removal and Resignation.** Any director may resign at any time by giving written notice to the Board of Directors, the President of the Corporation and/or Secretary; unless otherwise specified therein, the acceptance off such resignation shall not be necessary to make it effective. Any director may be removed, with or without cause, by the affirmative vote of a majority of the Board of Directors at a meeting of the Directors at which a quorum is present; provided, however, that a director may be removed only at a meeting called for the purpose of removing the Director, and the notice of such meeting shall state the purpose, or one of the purposes, is the Director removal. Any such resignation of removal shall take effect at the time specified therein.

D. **Annual Meetings.** The annual meeting of the Board of Directors shall be held in the month of January of each year, and shall be held for the purpose of electing new board members, electing new officers and transacting such other business as may come before the meeting.

E. **Special Meetings.** Special Board of Directors meetings may be called by or at the request of the President or by any two directors.

F. **Meetings.** Board of Directors meetings, regular or special, may be held at any place either within (name the state), or from time to time by resolution of the Board of Directors or by unanimous written consent of the members thereof. Board of Directors meetings shall be held upon such notice as provided herein. Neither the business to be transacted at, nor the purpose of, any regular or special Board of Directors meeting need be specified in the notice of waiver of notice of such meeting.

G. **Participation Through Electronic Communication.** Board of Directors members, or of any Board of Directors-designated committees, may participate in a Board of Directors meeting of Board of Directors committee meeting by means of conference telephone or similar communications equipment whereby all persons participating can hear each other, and participation in a meeting in this manner shall constitute presence in person at the meeting.

H. **Action Without Meeting.** Any action which is required to be or may be taken at a Board of Directors meeting, or a Board of Directors Committee meeting, may be taken without a meeting if consents in writing, settling forth the action so taken, are signed by all Board of Directors members or of the committee as the case may be. The consent shall have the same force and effect as a unanimous vote at the meeting duly held, and may be stated as such in any certificate of document. The Secretary shall file the consents with the Board of Directors meeting minutes or of the committee meeting minutes as the case may be.

I. **Notice.** Notice of any annual, regular or special meeting shall be given at least FIVE (5) days previous thereto by written notice delivered either personally, by facsimile, electronic mail, or other form of wire or wireless communication, or by mail to each Director at his or her business or home address. Written notice shall be deemed effective at the earlier of the following: (1) When received; (2) file days after its deposit in the US mail, as evidenced by the postmark, if mailed correctly and with first class postage affixed; or (3) on the date shown on the return receipt, if sent by registered or certified mail, return receipt requested, and the receipt is signed by or on behalf of the addressee. Any Director may waive notice of any meeting. The attendance of a director at any meeting shall constitute a waiver of notice of such meeting, except where a Director attends a meeting for the express purpose of objecting to the transaction of any business because the meeting is not lawfully called or convened. Neither the business to be transacted at, nor the purpose of, any regular or special Board of Directors meeting need be specified in the notice or waiver of notice of such meeting.

J. **Voting.** Each Director shall be entitled to one (1) vote on each matter submitted to a Board of Directors vote. A vote of a majority of the votes entitled to be cast by the Directors present at a meeting at which a quorum is present shall be necessary for the adoption of any matter voted upon by the Board of Directors.

K. **Quorum.** A Board of Directors majority shall constitute a quorum for the transaction of business at any Board of Directors meeting.

L. **Manner of Acting and Rules of Order.** In all matters not covered by the By-Laws, parliamentary procedures shall be governed by the manual knows as "Robert's Rules of Order, the Modern Edition." The act of the Board of Directors majority present at a Board of Directors meeting at which a quorum is present shall be the act of the Board of Directors, unless a greater number is required under the Articles of Incorporation, these By-Laws, any applicable (name of state) laws or Robert's Rules of Order.

M. **Number and Election.** The Corporation officers shall be a President, a Secretary/Treasurer. The Board of Directors may also elect a Vice President, Assistant Secretary and Assistant Treasurer. All officers shall be elected at the Board of Directors annual meeting by a majority of those Board members present, including newly-elected members, and said officers hall hold office at the pleasure of the Board of Directors until the next Annual meeting and until their successors shall have been elected and qualified. Where a vacancy occurs in an office, the Board of Directors shall fill the position for the unexpired term.

N. **President.** The President shall be the Corporation's chief executive officer. The President shall preside at all Board of Directors meetings and Board of Director Committee meetings and shall have the power to transact all of the usual, necessary and regular Corporation business as may be required and, with such prior Board authorization as may be required in these By-Laws to execute such contracts, deeds, bonds and other evidences of indebtedness, leases and other documents as shall be required by the Corporation; and, in general, shall perform all such other duties incident to the President's office and such other duties as the Board of Directors may prescribe from time to time.

O. **Secretary/Treasurer.** The Secretary/Treasurer shall record and preserve the Board of Directors and Committee meeting minutes, shall be responsible for authenticating Corporation records, shall cause notices of all Board of Directors meetings and committees to be given to the members thereof. Secretary/Treasurer shall be responsible for all Corporation funds shall direct that such funds be deposited in such bank or banks as Board of Directors may from time to time determine, and shall make reports to the Board of Directors as requested by the Board. The Secretary/Treasurer shall see that an accounting system is maintained in such a manner as to give a true and accurate accounting of the Corporation financial transactions, that reports of such transactions are presented promptly to the Board of Directors, that all expenditures are presented promptly to the Board of Directors, that all expenditures are made to the best possible advantage, and that all accounts payable are presented promptly for payment. The Secretary/Treasurer shall further perform such other duties incident to his or her office and as the Board of President may from time to time determine. If required by the Board of Directors, the Secretary/Treasurer shall give a bond for the faithful discharge of his or her duties in such sum and with such surety or sureties as the Board of Directors shall determine.

P. **Removal and Resignation.** Any officer may be removed, with or without cause, by the majority Board of Directors vote at any Board meeting. Any officer may resign at any time by giving written notice to the Board of Directors, the President or Secretary. Any such resignation or removal shall take effect at the time specified herein.

ARTICLE VI – GENERAL PROVISIONS

A. **Contracts, Etc. How Executed.** Except as in these Bylaws otherwise provided or restricted, the Board of Directors may authorize any officer or officers, agent or agents to enter into any contract or execute and deliver any instrument in the name of and on behalf of the Corp[oration, and such authority may be general or confined to specific instances; and, unless so authorized, no officer, agent or employee shall have any power or authority to bind the Corporation by any contract or engagement or to pledge its credit or to render it liable pecuniarily for any purpose or in any amount.

B. **Deposits.** All Corporation funds shall be deposited from time to time to the credit of the Corporation with such banks, bankers, trust companies or other depositories as the Board of Directors may select or as may be selected by any officer or officers, agent or agents of the Corporation to whom such power may be delegated from time to time by the Board of Directors.

C. **Checks, Drafts, etc.** All checks, drafts or other orders for the payment of money, notes, acceptances of other evidence of indebtedness issued in the name of the Corporation shall be signed by such officer of officers, agent or agents of the Corporation, and in such manner as shall be determined from time to time by Board of Directors resolution in accordance with the provisions of these Bylaws. Endorsements for deposit to the credit of the Corporation in any of its duly authorized depositories may be made without countersignature by the President or Secretary/Treasurer, or by any other officer of Corporation agent to whom the Board of Directors, by resolution, shall have delegated such power, or by hand-stamped impression in the name of the Directors.

ARTICLE VII – CONFLICT OF INTEREST

No contract or transaction between the Corporation and one or more of its Directors or officers, or between the Corporation and any other corporation, partnership, association, or organization in which one of more of its Directors or officers are Directors of officers, or have a financial interest, shall be void or voidable solely for that reason, or solely because the Director of officer is present at or participates in the meeting of the Board of committee thereof which authorizes the contract or transaction, or solely because his or her or their votes are counted for such purposes, if the material facts as to his or her relationship or interest and as to the contract or transaction are disclosed or are known to the Board of Directors or the committee, and the Board of committee in good faith, taking into account the fairness of the contract or transaction, authorizes the contract or transaction by the affirmative votes of a majority of the disinterested Directors present.

ARTICLE VIII – INDEMNIFICATION

A. **Mandatory indemnification.** The Corporation shall indemnify any Director who was wholly successful, on the merits or otherwise, in the defense of any proceeding to which the Director was a party because he or she is or was a Corporation Director against reasonable expenses actually incurred by the Director in connection with the proceeding.

B. **Permissive Indemnification.**

(1) The Corporation may indemnify any person who was or is a party or is threatened to be made a party to any threatened, pending or completed action, suit, or proceeding, whether civil, criminal, administrative or investigative, other than an action by or in the right of the Corporation, any reason of the fact that he or she is or was a Director, officer, employee or agent of the Corporation, or is or was serving at the request of the Corporation, or is or was serving at the request of the corporation as a Director, officer, employee or agent of another corporation, partnership, joint venture, trust or other enterprise, against expenses, including attorney fees, judgments, fines and amounts paid in settlement actually and reasonably incurred by him or her in connection with such action, suit, or process if he or she acted in good faith and in a manner he or she reasonably believed to be in or not opposed to the Corporation's best interests, and, with respect to any criminal action or proceeding, had no reasonable cause to believe his or her conduct was unlawful. The termination of any action, suit, or proceeding by judgment, by order, by settlement, by conviction, or upon a plea of nolo contendere or its equivalent, shall not, or itself, create a presumption that the person did not act in good faith and in a manner which he or she reasonably believed to be in or not opposed to the Corporation's best interests and, with respect to any criminal action or proceeding, that the person had reasonable cause to believe that his or her conduct was unlawful.

(2) The Corporation may indemnify any person who was or is a party or is threatened to be made a party to any threatened, pending or completed action or suit by or in the right of the Corporation to procure a judgment in its favor by reason of the fact that he or she is or was a Director, officer, employee or agent of the Corporation, or is or was serving at the request of the Corporation as a Director, officer, employee or agent of another

corporation, partnership, joint venture, trust or other enterprise against expenses, including attorney fees, and amounts paid in settlement actually and reasonably incurred by him or her in connection with the defense or settlement of the action or suit if he or she acted in good faith and in a manner he or she reasonably believed to be in or not opposed to the Corporation's best interests; except that no indemnification shall be made in respect of any claim, issue or matter as to which such person shall have been adjudged to be liable for negligence or misconduct in the performance of his or her duty to the Corporation unless and only to the extent that the court in which the action or suit was brought determines upon application that, despite the adjudication of liability and in view of all the circumstances of the case, the person is fairly and reasonably entitled to indemnification for such expenses for which the court shall deem proper.

(3) To the extent that a Director, officer, employee or agent of the Corporation has been successful on the merits or otherwise in defense of any action, suit, or proceeding referred to in subsections (1) and (2) of this section, or in defense of any claim, issue or matter therein, he or she shall be indemnified against expenses, including attorney fees, actually and reasonably incurred by him or her in connection with the action, suit or proceeding.

(4) Any indemnification under subsections (1) and (2) of this section, unless ordered by a court, shall be made by the Corporation only as authorized in the specific case upon a determination that indemnification of the Director, officer, employee or agent is proper in the circumstances because he or she has met the applicable standard of conduct set forth in this section. The determination shall be made by the Board of Directors by a majority vote of a quorum consisting of Directors who were not parties to the action, suit, or proceeding, or if such a quorum is not obtainable, or even if obtainable a quorum of disinterested Directors so directs, by independent legal counsel in a written opinion.

(5) Expenses incurred in defending a civil or criminal action, suit or proceeding may be paid by the Corporation in advance of the final disposition of the action, suit, or proceeding as authorized by the Board of Directors in the specific case upon receipt of an undertaking by or on behalf of the Director, officer, employee or agent to repay such amount

unless is hall ultimately be determined that he or she is entitled to be indemnified by the Corporation as authorized in this section.

(6) The indemnification provided by this section shall not be deemed exclusive of any other rights to which those seeking indemnification may be entitled under (state statute), any other provision of law, the Articles of Incorporation of the Corporation of these Bylaws or any agreement, vote of disinterested Directors or otherwise, both as to action in his or her official capacity and as to action in another capacity while holding such office, and shall continue as to a person who has ceased to be a Director, officer, employee or agent and shall inure to the benefit of the heirs, executors and administrators of such a person.

(7) The Corporation shall have the power to give any further indemnity, in addition to the indemnity authorized or contemplated under other subsections of this section, including subsection (6), to any person who is or was a Director, officer, employee or agent, or to any person who is or was serving at the request of the Corporation as a Director, officer, employee or agent of any other corporation, partnership, joint venture, trust or other enterprise, provided such further indemnity is either (i) authorized, directed or provided for in the Corporation Articles of Incorporation or any duly adopted amendment thereof, or (ii) is authorized, directed, or provided for in these Bylaws or agreement of the Corporation which has been adopted by a Board of Directors vote, and provided further that no such indemnity shall indemnify any person from or on account of such person's conduct which was finally adjudged to have been knowingly fraudulent, deliberately dishonest or willful misconduct.

(8) For the purpose of this section, references to the "Corporation" include all constituent corporations absorbed in a consolidation or merger as well as the resulting or surviving corporation so that any person who is or was a Director, officer, employee or agent of such a constituent corporation or is or was serving at the request of such constituent corporation as a Director, officer, employee or agent of another corporation, partnership, joint venture, trust or other enterprise shall stand in the same position under the provisions of this section with respect to the resulting or surviving corporation as he or she would if he or she had served the resulting or surviving corporation in the same capacity.

(9) For the purposes of this section, the term "other enterprise" shall include employee benefit plans; the term "fines" shall include any excise taxes assessed on a person with respect to an employee benefit plan; and the term "serving at the request of the Corporation" shall include any service as a Director, officer, employee or agent of the Corporation which imposes duties on, or involves services by, such Director, officer, employee, or agent with respect to an employee benefit plan, its participants, or beneficiaries; and a person who acted in good faith and in a manner he or she reasonably believed to be in the interest of the participants and beneficiaries of an employee benefit plan shall be deemed to have acted in a manner "not opposed to the best interests of the Corporation" as referred to in this section.

C. **Insurance.** The Corporation may purchase and maintain insurance on behalf of an individual who is or was a Director, officer, employee, or Corporation agent, or who, while a Director, officer, employee, or Corporation agent, is or was serving at the Corporation request as a Director, officer, partner, trustee, employee, or agent of another foreign or domestic business or nonprofit Corporation partnership, joint venture, trust, employee benefit plan, or other enterprise, against liability asserted against or incurred by him or her in that capacity or arising from his or her status as a Director, officer, employee, or agent, whether or not the Corporation would have power to indemnify the person against the same liability under section (A) or (B) above.

ARTICLE IX – AMENDMENTS TO ARTICLES AND BYLAWS

Any amendments to the Articles of Incorporation or the Corporation Bylaws must be approved by the Board of Directors.

(Name)

Incorporator

_____

SEE WHAT I MEAN?

I forget how long it took for our club planning team to go through and decide some of these Bylaw sections, and that was after a few years of testing and practicing on how we wanted to operate. So again, **don't jump into adopting Bylaws.** First get some knowledge—visit that friendly attorney I've been referring to—and get some experience running your desired club to help you define how you want to operate. Then you will be in a better place to design Bylaws.

You will thank me later. Or start drinking early, as one beekeeping president told me!

ADD COSTS TO YOUR PROJECTED CLUB EXPENSES

After getting established and knowing how and why you want to be a bee club, **fundraise** for the cost of formally incorporating. The cost will vary but for planning purposes you will need at least $500 to get formal **Bylaws and Articles of Incorporation.**

Not counting any coffee. Or alcohol.

Your Notes

_____

_____

_____

_____

Your Notes

_____

_____

_____

_____

_____

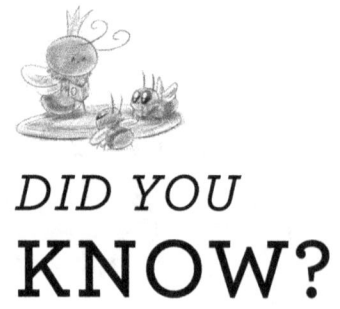

DID YOU KNOW?

- The perfect hexagons that form honeycomb hold the most amount of honey with the smallest amount of material (wax).

- In order to make a pound of honey, a honey bee colony must fly 55,000 miles.

(Courtesy of Beepods.com)

- In 2017, the top honey producing states were North Dakota, South Dakota, and California.

(Courtesy of statista.com)

CHAPTER 6

Bee Club Leadership

"If you need something from some body always give that person a way to hand it to you."

— Sue Monk Kidd, (1940-present)
The Secret Life of Bees, an author who listened to honeybees in her home walls.

Leadership is about **setting expectations as well as the tone.** As you set up your bee club, make sure to say "thank you." A lot. Thank people for coming. Thank helpers for what they are doing. Thank your supporters publicly. **Recognize people like spouses** who are often the unsung heroes in these kinds of organizations. First and foremost, remember to do, and **be, kind. Always.**

HOW BIG A CLUB?

How big a club you develop is based on two things:
- what you are **trying to accomplish**
- what **your volunteers** are willing to do.

*Make it clear what needs to be done at club meetings and **welcome volunteers** to "chair" the various jobs. On second thought, just be thankful for any help, the term "chairing" can be scary to some people. See if calling it "adult supervision" works better!*

In general, **smaller clubs are better.** The smaller size ensures people get to know each other. Club participants can support each other once they get acquainted. Volunteers are willing to pitch in because the work is relatively easy.

In addition, beekeeping conditions vary. Having a group of people from the same area will help with quickly **sharing information** and **dealing with similar conditions.** And conditions can **vary from city to city and microclimates.**

WHAT DO YOU WANT TO ACCOMPLISH?

To think about this another way, **what does success look like** when you end your time with the club. After all, you want some way to gauge that your time made a difference, don't you? Every leader **should have goals** for their time in their position.

- Goals help keep the leaders on the **right path.**
- It also **makes it easier** to decide whether you want to take something on.
- If it helps the group reach their goal, then **give it some thought.** If not, move on to the next item or set it aside for later.

Most goals come from the **organization's leadership.** The three or four officers each contribute to moving the group forward by doing their respective jobs.

WHAT IF YOU DISAGREE?

Before you start complaining, make sure you **understand the focus and purpose of the group. If you disagree** with the group's premise:

- Club officers are legally responsible for meeting the club's legal requirements. Look into the issue and understand **why they do what they do** before you disagree; they may be doing what is required of them.
- Sometimes something is done a certain way because that is the only way the person in the position knows how to do it. **Offer to help them** with the job; teach them options. Volunteer to help.
- Clearly state your concern and why. Include recommendations for one or more alternative or alternative approaches. Volunteer to do what you recommend. **Be part of the solution, not the problem.**

PRAISE IN PUBLIC, PROBLEM SOLVE IN PRIVATE

If you are in a leadership position, there are those situations when something goes wrong and the individuals involved have to be addressed. My Navy experience taught me the principle of **discussing it in private** and **praising in public.** Actually this applies to most things in an organization or life, in general.

As a leader **you are setting the example.** If you want to resolve the issue:

- Concentrate on addressing it with the immediate individual(s) as **soon as possible.** If you do it quietly, the parties involved can save face and make amends.
- If they don't cooperate, they can be **asked to/agree to leave.** You want people who are contributing to your community, not draining it.
- Even when you have the uncomfortable conversation in private, remember to **thank them** for their contributions both personally and in public.

In today's contentious society, some people like the drama of taking disagreements public. It is much easier to make your life difficult than for them to acknowledge a mistake and make an effort to fix it. If you are attacked:

- **Be honest and open** about what is happening.
- **Acknowledge the issue and that options** have been provided to resolve them.
- **Stick to the high road.** The people with the issues may continue to make things difficult but, in the end, others will decide what to believe and who to trust. If you **are consistent** with what you said you were doing, it will work out.

BEING QUEEN

In most organizations there are "official" leaders and unofficial ones.

- **The official leaders** are the ones with the titles, legally responsible for certain specified duties and who, at least on paper, hold each other accountable.

- **The unofficial leaders** are the ones who may not have a title but through experience, relationships and successful accomplishments hold sway over the group and get things done. Just as in a hive, the queen bee lays eggs and sets the tone but it is the worker bees that get the work of the colony done.

However, just as in a hive not everyone gets to be queen bee, **not everyone** is cut out to be a leader. The one most reliable, and relatable trait is that the members have to accept, support and follow the person in leadership.

Although I know a number of excellent leaders who could care less about titles, they also know the titles, and the position, are not for, or about them. **When one fills a leadership position,** decisions then switch from **what is in the best interest of the individual to what is best for the organization.**

Some positions are required by law to make it clear who is legally responsible for what part of the organization. The outline of responsibilities also makes it clear who to talk to about related issues as well as who is held accountable for getting that done. Most duties are found **described in Bylaws**. This is a **bare bones description** of club leadership roles and how they work together:

PRESIDENT

The president has the **long-range view,** making sure the club is headed in the right direction. The president often tweaks the club's mission based on past successes and future goals all designed to support the club's main mission.

- The focus of this position is to find good people and to make sure the others **are working out well in their positions and with each other.**
- **The president has the organization's best interests in mind, not his/her interests.** Even if the president doesn't like legalities or details, the president follows the laws and checks details because this is now about making sure the club is working well. Most groups need both policies and procedures to work smoothly.

The most important selection this person makes is the vice president, who often succeeds the president.

VICE PRESIDENT

Most vice presidents focus on the **day-to-day operations**, making sure deadlines get met, required reports get filed and conflicts get quickly resolved.

- This is the position with the short-term view, focused on **keeping momentum going.**
- It's also an excellent position to train for the presidency because this person develops an understanding of the mission and knows how the club operates.

It is critical for the **president and vice president to work closely together** since they both bring something different but complimentary to the club.

However, people who are used to tracking details can be challenged to move into the "longer range" presidential position because they are no longer in charge of the details and have to depend on others to get the work done. **If this leadership team can sort out what needs to be done and divide the workload among themselves, that can work, too.**

SECRETARY

The secretary is the one who **keeps the club records** from meeting notes to historic files and documents.

- This can be an easy job if the **person running the meeting** runs the meeting well and decisions are clearly stated and understood. However, if the person running the meeting doesn't follow the meeting agenda or clearly manages how decisions are made, this can be a very challenging position. It can open the club up to political gamesmanship as members try to alter previous decisions they don't support.
- The best defense is to have **good job descriptions** and **clear notes.**

TREASURER

The treasurer is the **money person**, collecting and making payments while **keeping records** of how the money came in and was spent. There are a lot of items on the board's agenda to make motions to accept and vote on.

- **The treasurer's report should not be one of them.**
- The treasurer's report should be acknowledged and **filed with the secretary for audit.**

PAST PRESIDENT

Whenever I am thinking of volunteering at an organization, this is one of the people I contact with my questions. The past president is **the mentor** for the incoming vice president and president. This person can be **most influential** because of established relationships and knowledge picked up in earlier positions.

GOOD SUCCESSION PLANNING

All of these positions are excellent training venues for **future club leadership.** Some start as secretary or treasurer, then move up the positions, building on what they learned in the previous job. Make sure you have a clear way volunteers can move through the positions so that you maintain **leadership continuity.**

EXECUTIVE COMMITTEE

In most organizations, the Executive Committee is made up of the four officers – president, vice president, secretary, treasurer and at times, the past president as an advisor. Together, this is the group that is **legally responsible and accountable** for club activities.

BOARD OF DIRECTORS

The Board of Directors – I sometimes refer to them as just the Board – decide on **long-range club policies and procedures.** They may also be asked to settle policy disputes and contribute to club planning. In some states, some club officers are also allowed to be Board members.

As you start your bee club, start small and build so if you can have club officers doubling on the board, do so. **Add more people** after you have a solid foundation.

WHO SHARES INFORMATION FIRST

This is important in general. It is even more important if you are **in a leadership position.** You are representing the group and regardless of how you are information-sharing, you will be perceived in most cases as a trustworthy information source.

- If you have something to share, **double check details** before sharing.
- **Only share** if it is something **within your responsibility**.
- If you have heard something about someone else, make some calls if you must quietly confirm but **let them share their news in their own time.** In most cases, the information you hear about someone else is mostly wrong. Give people a chance to get their details pulled together before they say anything. It's similar to you telling your family your sister is pregnant before she's had a chance to spring the news on her own terms in her own time.
- If you're information is incorrect, quickly corrext it. Once you lose trust it's very hard to regain and can take a very long time if it's even possible. Remember **you represent your club now.**

RUNNING A MEETING

First, decide if you even need a meeting. The majority of club functions can be handled through phone calls, texts, emails so only set meetings when you need to **set new policy, direction and plan.** If you need to **trouble-shoot,** focus on including who will **contribute to solving the issue.**

Be organized. There are few things more frustrating, and that will make volunteers disappear, than to have a **disorganized, confusing and hard to follow meetings** that lasts longer than it should because no one knows what is going on. Or maybe that's just me but nevertheless. To effectively run a meeting:

- If you are just starting, **develop a meeting agenda** with a set time frame.
- **Start** your meetings **on time.**
- **End** your meetings **on time.**

- If you are taking over, **get the minutes** from the last previous meetings and develop an agenda.

SAMPLE BASIC MEETING AGENDA

A. Note date, time, location, who was in attendance.

B. STANDING REPORTS:

    Secretary: Last meeting's minutes

    Treasurer's report

C. OLD BUSINESS (pending items from past meetings)

    List a summary of the issue, who has details to share.

D. NEW BUSINESS (new topics)

E. STANDING COMMITTEE REPORTS

F. Next meeting (date, time, location)

CLEARLY SHOW WHAT NEEDS TO BE DECIDED

Some meeting agenda items are good to know, others require decisions. Some people need information, and time to decide so make sure your agenda goes out **7-10 days** before your meeting to give people **time to prepare**.

It is also helpful to make it clear on the agenda which items will **require a decision**. One way to make that clear is to mark each presentation:

- For information
- For majority vote decision
- For majority vote sensing and then president makes final decision.

Actually, the **president is held accountable** regardless but some people like to get a good discussion going and **get a sense** for how the whole group feels about an issue. The discussion is a good way to **get buy-in** into a decision as well. Just make sure everyone knows this is discussion-only before you get started or some people will misunderstand why they didn't get to vote.

HOW DECISIONS ARE MADE

Most U.S. organizations follow **Robert's Rules of Order.** You will find the actual book in most public libraries as well as cheat sheets easily online. Basically someone makes a proposal; another person agrees to the proposal and seconds it; the person running the meeting calls for discussion; then there is another proposal for a vote; another person agrees and seconds, and then there is a vote. Sounds simple enough until someone misuses a critical term so here is the correct way to end a discussion:

- **"Tabling"** means you are ending any further discussion on a proposal never to be brought back up again.
- **"Setting aside"** means there needs to be further discussion at a future date so the current discussion will stop until a future date.

When misused and included in meeting minutes, something that should have had more discussion can be inadvertently killed off so if you **don't remember the correct terms, don't use them.** Say instead "we will come back to this later" or "we won't talk about this proposal again" so the intent is clearly documented in meeting notes.

ALTERNATIVES TO ROBERT'S RULES OF ORDER

Okay, so you're not a fan. Not a problem, there are plenty of other **excellent small meeting guides** to keep you on track:

- Ignore Robert's Rules Thing https://bit.ly/BCB-Roberts-Rules
- Law of Order: Key Terms: https://bit.ly/KeyTerms-LOO
- Beginner's Guide to Governing Documents https://bit.ly/LOO-docs
- Going for Consensus, Not Robert's Rules https://bit.ly/NotRobertsRules
- Martha's Rules of Order https://bit.ly/MarthasROO

COMMUNICATING YOUR MEETING PLANNING

To be effective participants, people need **advance notice** on what is expected of them at a meeting. They also need advance notice to participate in the meeting planning.

One way to be efficient as well as effective is to set up a calendar of when participants can expect emails from you:

- **Right after a meeting** (within 3 days) with a summary of decisions made.
- **Two weeks prior** to the next meeting, asking for meeting topics
- **Ten days prior** to the meeting, sharing meeting agenda as well as secretary's notes from the last meeting and treasurer's report.
- **Two days prior** to meeting, meeting reminder.

Discuss what your **team needs** and **be consistent** with how and when you share information.

YIKES, WHAT TO WRITE!

When you are in a leadership position, you will have the opportunity to keep nudging your goals through **newsletters**. Most have columns from the president, providing a forum for the group leader to – well, go bonkers trying to think up what to write. After which they desperately try to find someone else to do it for them and. Wait, this is not that hard. And what a great opportunity to put **your emphasis** on the things your team is getting done.

Most of us have written those newsy family Christmas letters at one time or another, and how many of us text event details every day. A newsletter column is just a shorter, or longer version with some fact checking before it is published. Think of it as a **billboard** for what your organization is doing.

Studies show people have to hear something **7-10 times** before it sinks in. If you mention an item in your column, then it's brought up and highlighted in other newsletter sections, at meetings and through social media reminders...No guarantees but now you just may get through the noise of life.

So the deadline to get your column finished is coming up, **what do you write about?**

- First, think about who is going to read the newsletter. Usually you will have members, advertisers and partners. What **information would they like to have?**
- Review the draft newsletter to see **what everyone else has submitted**, that will give you a menu of possible topics to mention.
- **Highlight upcoming activities.** What is the next thing your group is doing after the newsletter goes out? Talk about event details and how members can participate. What time, where, is there a special fee for members and nonmembers?
- If you went to the event last year, **mention something** about that experience. If this is a new event, thank those who pulled it together. Do they still need help?
- **Give shout outs** to the people who make things happen. When mentioning an event, include at least 2 names of people associated with each event and say something nice about what they are doing. People still **love to see their name in print.**
- When I was a newspaper editor, I remember running into a lady who insisted on introducing me to her whole family as the woman who got her name "in the newspaper." Later when I checked, I was surprised to find her name in a police report, she had been cited for speeding. I had to give it to her, though, she was "in the newspaper!"
- **Identify opportunities** where others can get involved. Whatever the event is, invite people to help. **List specifically** how people can get involved, who to contact, what is the time frame for volunteering. Sometimes people hesitate to volunteer because they want first to know what is expected of them.
- If the event is designed especially for members, **say so.** Explain who asked for it and how the event will address whatever they requested. This demonstrates your club is being responsive to the community you are trying to build.
- **Add a photo of yourself.** It can be as simple as you smiling into the camera or something you have a friend take at a meeting. Tie it to your club position so people can recognize you when they see you. They will also be more tempted to **contact you** with suggestions or issues if they feel they know you.

- **Mark special holidays** with a personal note.
    - Thank a spouse for an upcoming anniversary or wish everyone a safe Thanksgiving. You want to be approachable and to show people you also **enjoy the same things** they may be enjoying.
    - Besides the standard holidays, you can **celebrate something specific** to your club. For example, May 20 is World Bee Day. **Check for bee-related special days websites** for suggested wording and fun facts.

MONTHLY MEETING PLANNING CHECKLIST

WHEN	X	WHAT	WHO	NOTES
End Meeting		Next meeting date & time		
		Guest speaker/demos/topics		
		Thank You		
Review		What went well		
		What needs to be changed		
		What needed for next month		
		Anything needed for 2 months from now?		
3 Weeks Prior		Speakers Confirmed		
		Meeting notices posted		
2 Weeks Prior		Purchase needed supplies		
		Discuss demos with presenters		

1 Week Prior		Send newsletter with meeting info/reminder		
		Confirm demos		
		• ID equipment needed for speakers and demos • Practice online meeting		
Day Before		Pack up demo equipment		
		Door Prizes		
		Thank you honey jars		
Meeting Day		Greeters		
		Refreshments		
		Demos		
		Presenters		
		Special Thank You to		
		Next meeting date and topics reminder		
		• Safety • Location of bathrooms/exits • Where to go in the event of an emergency such as a tornado • Who the local medics are • Where cords are and how they are marked off • Is there cell service • Water source • First Aid Kit • EpiPen®		

LEADERSHIP CHALLENGES

An effective bee club will need **honest, caring people** to be sustainable so here are some of the **main leadership challenges** a new bee club may face.

A. **Get good advice.** The initial bee club planning team will benefit from experience from other club managers. They need not be beekeepers so **tap people** who have successful clubs and invite them to meet with your planning team. Take their advice and suggestions.

B. **Planning team members with differing agendas.** Whether it is one member who wants to make money and another member who wants only to educate beekeepers, it is important that the bee club planning team **have the same goals** and is headed in the **same direction.**

- Laws require that groups with assets have a **clearly outlined way to dispose of club assets** in the event the bee club is disbanded. Use a Club Charter specifying how the planning group intends to operate. Include how assets will be disposed of and have every planning team member agree, sign and date it.

- If someone doesn't sign it, they should not be part of the planning committee or there could be a **tendency to derail the group plans** to get the assets.

- Check with an attorney and certified public accountant to make sure you are setting up your organization and properly documenting, even the basic ones. It will be easier to do it earlier than to re-do it later. Ask any established club about their experience trying to change hastily-developed Bylaws and then re-read this section. Twice.

C. **Money.** Most bee clubs I have been involved with have had issues at one time or another with money. It is the **founder and/or club president's responsibility** to make sure the funds are accounted for and well managed with the help of the treasurer.

- **Don't blame the treasurer later** if you haven't made the treasurer regularly give an account on funds to the bee club planning team. Do this from the start. Develop early good habits.

- To ensure there is no question, the **treasurer should be the only one** collecting, tracking, spending and reporting on the status of funds, even if pressured publicly to "guess" at amounts in the treasury.
- If someone is assisting in money collection, make sure all funds collected are accountable **by a second person and in writing after the meeting.** That way there is **no question later** and all parties are held accountable.
- Have **two people signing** on the bee club bank accounts so the treasurer has a back-up and doesn't tie up bee club activities in his/her absence.

D. **Fundraising Challenges.** Sometimes bee clubs need to pursue fundraisers to generate a basic treasury to fund some of their activities.

- **Make sure the plan is clear,** funds are earmarked and that all funds are provided to the treasurer. People tend to pitch in if they know what they have to do and how the money will be spent.
- If the fundraiser comes up short, **do a postmortem** to determine what went wrong and revise before pursuing again.
- Before proceeding, **contact fundraiser supply providers** to make sure all original information was accurate.
- **Don't make commitments** to fundraisers without the advance approval of the planning team and without having final expected funds accountability.
- The decision to hold a fundraiser should be **made by the bee club planning committee** so everyone is behind the activity.
- Check with a certified public accountant on any taxable related activities and reporting requirements.

E. **Special Privilege Expectations.** When running an educational nonprofit bee club, **no one person should financially benefit from their club position.** A club can lose their nonprofit IRS status if club members don't manage the club in the designated format. If an event makes money, the funds go into the club treasury, not back to the fundraising planners, the club officers and/or individual club volunteers. The following are some of the more **common special privilege expectations** and suggestions **on how to manage them:**

- **Bee Club t-shirts.** Find a commercial outlet and let individuals buy their own. It's expensive to buy and store them and a challenge to keep a variety of sizes on hand.
- **Bee Club patches.** Good alternative to t-shirts. Work with a local embroidery shop to design and sell those so people can easily add them to t-shirts, hats, vests and so forth **without a big club investment.**
- **Paid conference expenses.** Most beginning bee clubs don't have funds to cover this so if you want to offer this, budget for it. Once you have funds, place your **bee club attendee names in a hat** and whoever is selected understands their expenses are being paid in return for them reporting back to the bee club at a future meeting.
- **Taking items from a group purchase for free.** Not acceptable unless everyone gets a free item.
- **Officers keep bee club purchased beekeeping books to "loan" out to area beekeepers.** That has the perception of a conflict of interest and creates a burden for the members with the books. Instead **donate beekeeping books to a local library** and have them manage who checks them out.
- **Officers sell items to the club, have the club collect the money and get paid for the items.** This is **illegal on two counts.** First, someone selling items needs to charge and collect taxes and secondly, they should be reporting income from the sales. If the club does this for them, the club becomes **party to tax evasion. Not the kind of party you want to have!**
- **Club members have the club market and sell their products without the club having liability insurance.** If something happens to the buyer, then club officers are liable for damages. If someone who attends a meeting wants to mention what they sell, that's up to the individual. Be careful of doing anything that **may appear** to be a club endorsement.
- **Someone asks if club members sell bees.** Invite them to a club meeting so they can meet area beekeepers and make their own contacts on potential bee sources. Be careful to not recommend someone else's products or you will be endorsing their products and taking on the liability.

F. **Working with Kids.** Many volunteer groups working with kids under 18 years of age now **require background checks** for the safety of the underaged participants. The checks also protect the individual associating with the kids. There's an **expense, and waiting period,** to get these background checks. Some organizations will not allow anyone to work with kids without a background check so ask what requirements they have.

G. **Liability Insurance.** It is a good idea to include in your bee club budget the annual cost for liability insurance for board members and sponsored events. After shopping around, we found the best reasonably priced policy with a farm-related insurance agency costing around $350/year.

H. **Donate Books to Local Library.** One of the services a local bee club can provide to the local beekeeping community is to **fundraise to buy and donate** beekeeping reference books to the local public library.

- Check what is **currently available** on the shelves, then meet with the head librarian to find out if they have a wish list for beekeeping books. Select books that do not duplicate what the library has and provide information for both beginning as well as experienced beekeepers.
- Also suggest that the library carry a subscription to **two beekeeping magazines**: Bee Culture and American Bee Journal, and you can also sponsor those subscriptions by paying for them. Most libraries allow magazines to be checked out for 1-2 weeks.
- Making the books easily available through a local public library **reduces the club workload** and **makes books easily accessible.**

I. **What's In a Name.** Sometimes asking someone to be "in charge" can be scary. Start with the "ask" and explain you need help with something specific. As they understand and become more comfortable with the role, then move them into a leadership position. If they've been comfortably and successfully involved in other efforts, it's easier to ask them to lead something right off the bat but don't assume someone can do it well. Have them demonstrate how they can contribute first.

J. **Other leadership challenges?** Michelle Colopy, executive director of LEAD for Pollinators, Inc. has an excellent blog covering management issues. She also offers online classes that may be helpful as well as leadership training. And she's a beekeeper. https://leadforpollinators.org/leadership/

Your Notes

_____

_____

_____

_____

_____

_____

_____

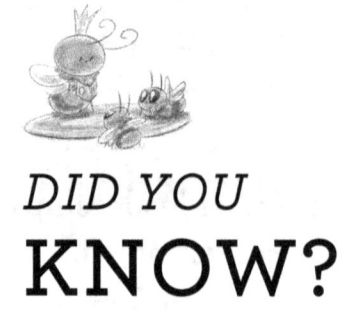

DID YOU KNOW?

- In the US, more than 300 different kinds of honey are produced every year. The variety in color and flavor is determined by the types of flowers from which the bees collect nectar.

- Every bee colony has its own distinct scent so that members can identify each other.

- Honey bees have 170 odorant receptors and a sense of smell 50 times more powerful than a dog.

(Courtesy of Beepods.com)

CHAPTER 7

Conflicts of Interest

"Financial planners who take commissions have a built-in conflict of interest... even with disclosure, my choice would be a fee-only planner."

— *Jane Bryant Quinn, U.S. columnist and financial advisor*

If there is one issue that many clubs and associations struggle with it is the idea of "conflicts of interest." In simplest terms, a conflict of interest is when **club leadership, which are voting officers and board members, are getting more out of the relationship than the club and association is getting.**

To make it clear to everyone what is acceptable, clubs should have a **written conflict-of- interest policy.** A conflict-of-interest policy includes:

- A requirement for board members to **annually disclose** personal and professional affiliations.
- It also sets forth a **process to follow** when considering a **business relationship with a board member.**

*When I decided to start writing beekeeping books, I moved from **a voting to an advisory position** on our state beekeeping association. Even though they didn't have a conflict of interest policy, being an advisor kept me separate from any potential decision-making that may have involved me and/or my books.*

The conflict-of-interest policy can be included in board minutes and/or developed as part of the Club Charter and/or Bylaws. **The key is to have a permanent written record** of how the club is operating and **what is, and isn't, accepted.** The written policy helps to dispel issues later on, especially as officers and board members turn over and new people come on board. As you develop your conflict-of-interest policy, there are two key aspects to consider: **personal benefits** and **self-dealing.**

CONFLICT OF INTEREST: PERSONAL BENEFITS

Personal benefit, or private inurement, is **prohibited in all nonprofits.** Private inurement is when a club member who has a significant influence over the club, such as a voting officer, voting board member, family member, major donor - **enters into an arrangement and receives benefits greater than he or she provides.**

How do you determine a person's contribution versus what they get out of their club association? One of the easiest ways I have used to clearly identify an individual's focus is to **look at their volunteer hours.**

The Independent Sector sets a **yearly value** for nonprofit volunteer hours, which at this writing is $28.54 an hour. How many hours has the individual volunteered? What is the **monetary value** from that person's donated time? If they are getting more out of the relationship than they are contributing then they are personally benefitting. That's not a formal formula but it is one of the **quickest ways** to easily assess if you have a conflict-of-interest situation.

CONFLICT OF INTEREST: SELF-DEALING

The other key conflict of interest principle is when a **person is on both sides of a financial transaction.** In a nonprofit organization, self-dealing may happen when the organization does business with a voting officer and/or voting board member.

- **Self-dealing in itself is not illegal** to all nonprofits.
- It is best handled with a written policy of **how business will be conducted** with club leadership.
- One of the givens in that policy is that the voting club officers and/or board members **excuse themselves from the vote on the proposed business that involves them.**

- If you're thinking you can get around this issue by setting up a private foundation, think again. **Private foundations are strictly forbidden** from engaging in such activities, no matter how insignificant the monetary benefit.

APPEARANCE OF CONFLICTS OF INTEREST

Sometimes the appearance of a conflict of interest can have **similar implications** as an actual conflict of interest. The best way to prevent this from developing is to **keep all discussions above board, in the open,** and **documented in meeting minutes**. If something seems questionable, get a board vote and enter it into the record.

- If someone asks about an issue, **address it promptly**. Sometimes the appearance of a conflict develops because someone is new and doesn't know the history.
- Allegations of a conflict of interest can also surface from jealousy and other board politics. **Nip it in the bud.** You want club members to trust what you are doing, not spend time gossiping and speculating on what they may or may not have heard.

BAD CONDUCT

Bad conduct is one of the **increasingly difficult issues** to manage with paid employees let alone volunteers. More organizations are now asking volunteers to agree to **written codes of conduct** to address some of the more difficult societal issues. Similar to the written club charters, the code of conduct should spell out **expectations and consequences** for unacceptable behavior. Consult an attorney about how to effectively address this especially if you start having complaints.

This is a **sample annual volunteer code of conduct** for a public university volunteer group. I have it here to give you an idea what goes into some of these codes of conduct, which include legal requirements as well as good business practices. Note what they say about conflicts of interest – basically **don't have any!**

SAMPLE VOLUNTEER ANNUAL CODE OF CONDUCT

Volunteers are key partners, helping guide and deliver programs that matter to (state) citizens. The university depends and expects all volunteers to understand and uphold the following Volunteer Code of Conduct at all times while serving as a volunteer.

BE ACCOUNTABLE TO AND WORK WITHIN THE UNIVERSITY SYSTEM

1. Work within the scope of assigned volunteer role and follow all related program policies and procedures.

2. Conduct behavior in strict accordance with applicable laws and confidential information policies, using confidential information only as needed to perform volunteer duties. The following rules apply:

    a. access confidential information only with proper approval and refrain from misusing or treating it carelessly;

    b. do not divulge, copy, release, sell, loan, review, alter or destroy any confidential information except as properly authorized;

    c. understand and agree that any violation of the responsibilities explained in this section subjects a volunteer to discipline, possible removal from the volunteer role or legal liability.

    What is meant by confidentiality? Confidential information means personal information of another person, which includes home addresses, telephone numbers, social security numbers, birth dates, etc. Also, do not include personal contact information of another in newsletters and announcements without their expressed consent.

3. Treat all youth and adults equally, without discrimination. This includes providing equal access to participation for all youth and adults, regardless of race, color, sex, pregnancy, national origin, ancestry, sexual orientation, gender identity, gender expression, religion, age, veteran status, disability, or any other status protected by applicable federal or state law. Sexual violence is also prohibited, including but not limited to sexual misconduct, sexual exploitation, sex-based stalking, and dating/intimate partner violence.

4. Avoid harming youth or adults, whether through sexual harassment, physical force, verbal or mental abuse or neglect. Retaliation for making or supporting a report of discrimination or harassment is also prohibited.

5. If your volunteer responsibilities meet the definition of a mandated reporter (i.e. anyone with care, custody or control of a child), then assume the role of a mandated reporter and, if concerned a child has been/or will be abused and/or neglected, contact the child abuse hotline. If it appears the child is in imminent danger, contact law enforcement as well.

When am "I" a Mandated Reporter? If youth are registered participants in a program, you are responsible to report suspected symptoms of child abuse and neglect even if parents are present. Exception: When a school visits, the teacher in charge of the group is the mandated reporter.

6. Avoid conflict of interest between assigned volunteer role(s) and personal business interests.

BE A POSITIVE ROLE MODEL AT ALL TIMES

1. Obey all laws of the locality, state and nation, including laws against forgery, theft, destruction or defacement of property.

2. Display mutual respect to others, practicing patience, cooperation and teamwork.

3. Practice personal and intellectual integrity.

4. Under no circumstances engage in unlawful manufacture, distribution, dispensation, possession, or use of a controlled substance at any club event. Avoid unlawful possession, use and/or distribution of alcohol at any club event. Avoid misuse or abuse of prescribed or over-the-counter drugs.

5. Be respectful of diverse opinions and perspectives.

6. Actively promote a safe environment for participants, volunteers, visitors, staff and others involved in the program.

Please consider volunteering as a privilege, not a right. Adhering to the code of conduct ensures the safety and protection of all, including yourself. Additionally, you have the authority to report abuses of the code of conduct to your supervisor. Failure to uphold any of the code of conduct standards above may result in coaching by a supervisor. Depending on the severity, this may include reassignment, role restriction and, if appropriate, removal from all volunteer roles. As representatives of the club, we have a shared responsibility to watch out for one another and to ensure the code of conduct is being followed.

END OF SAMPLE VOLUNTEER ANNUAL CODE OF CONDUCT

Your Notes

_____

_____

_____

_____

_____

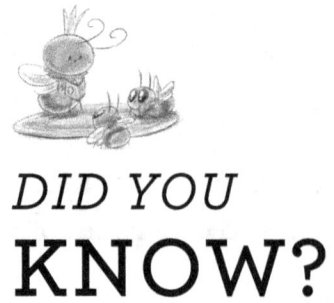

DID YOU **KNOW?**

- The oldest know art depicting honey gathering can be found in the Cave of the Spider near Valencia, Spain.
- The ancient Greeks and Romans viewed honey as a symbol of love, beauty, and fertility.
- Beekeeping is said to be the second oldest profession.

(Courtesy of Beepods.com)

CHAPTER 8

Managing Bee Club Volunteers

"Gracious words are a honeycomb, sweet to the soul and healing to the bones."
— *Proverbs 16:24, English Standard Bible*

Nonprofit volunteer organizations **depend on voluteers** but some don't appreciate what they have. One of the events I volunteered to help with reminded me of a very basic principle that applies to anything we do together: listen, value what is offered to you and **don't yell** at people to try to make them do what you want them to do instead. If you ever were a parent, how did that work for you?

Precisely.

In this case, what was being demanded was not only illegal but proven time and again to be ineffectual. However, for some people who are poor leaders, demanding volunteers do things without regard to price and outcome is more important than the success of the event. Ironically enough, the volunteers brought the level of professional background and expertise that were necessary for the event's success. Once I met some of the other team members, they said they just nodded and worked around the ridiculous demands, proving yet again that if you have **good volunteers who know what they are doing** and what the organization is trying to accomplish, they can **make anything a success.**

*Encourage people to bring **"show and tell" items** to share and discuss at club meetings such as beekeeping tools and photos of bee behavior. In photo, sample hive feeders with emphasis on inside hive feeding. Oops, I forgot one, now where's my hummingbird feeder!*

GETTING VOLUNTEERS

There is a simple way to get volunteers for most anything, from running for office to establishing a bee club: **Ask.**

When you are first starting, you will have a group of people who "want to help" so spend time together discussing **what needs to be done** and engaging volunteers in specific duties. As you evolve:

- **Have clearly defined duties/**functions someone can do. Write a job description. Share widely.
- **Observe.** After a few club meetings you will start seeing some of the same faces at meetings. Ask them to stay afterwards to clean up or suggest they take on something for a next meeting.
- **Reach out to people** you know have certain skills and ask them to help. You may need to negotiate how much time they can contribute or when they can volunteer so be flexible.
- **Accept help.** Be open to suggestions and ideas, and accept what someone is offering.

Once your structure is established, **keep a list of duties and opportunities** posted on your website so people can easily find out how they can be involved.

- Sometimes a group that has been together for some time will seem intimidating to new arrivals. Remember to periodically **invite people to volunteer,** and mention the things that need to be done.
- In all volunteer positions, **build a back-up** so the lead person has someone who can fill in if they are not available. Again, this is another way to encourage people working together, build community and prevent others from burning out.

BE SPECIFIC ABOUT WHAT HELP YOU NEED

There are a number of **basic club functions**. In some situations, one person can bundle some of these together but try to share the load so that the work doesn't fall on just one or two people. **Having more people working** together is also how you build, and expand, your community.

Here are the basics you need starting:

1. **Meeting Logistics.** Someone needs to make meeting location arrangements, either for an in-person meeting and/or for online meetings.
2. **Refreshments.** If meeting in person during COVID virus pandemic, keep this simple and package servings individually.
3. **Greeters.** Welcome people to your meeting, have a sign in sheet to identify who attended and who you can contact for future meetings.
4. **Program Chair.** This person coordinates meeting presentations.
5. **Tech Support.** Helpful especially for those online meetings, identify someone who knows what online platforms you are using and how to manage them.

Once the club is established and you are growing, you may need to **select more positions to fill.** Here's a more complete possible list of jobs:

1. **Bee Wranglers.** Love this term for the people who are responsible for getting bees for, and to, a particular event.
2. **Club Ambassadors.** These can be young beekeepers and past club presidents who continue to support club activities.
3. **Communications.** This is the person who manages the club's information-sharing. They are usually a board member and are responsible for a consistent message and image across the various platforms.
4. **Community Relations.** Once it's known you have a club, there will be ongoing requests for everything from tours to manning event booths and giving lectures. This person can collect the information and manage whether the requests are something your club is ready to support.
5. **Fundraisers.** Especially as you start, it will be helpful to have someone planning, working and keeping tabs on events that help your club raise operating funds. They can collect ideas from others but one person should be tracking all opportunities.
6. **Greeters.** These are the volunteers who welcome people to the meeting, sign them up and answer questions one-on-one. This is a good place to start new volunteers and is an excellent way to make people feel welcomed.

7. **Medical Support.** This person comes in handy at hands on demonstrations and can assist if there is an incident.

8. **Meeting Logistics.** Reserving space, finding the chairs, getting location requirements and restrictions, confirming use, making sure there is enough parking and such. It's helpful in this position to have someone who is good at details and thinking things through. **The same applies to online meetings.** Select a platform everyone is comfortable learning and using. Plan dress rehearsals to minimize online glitches.

9. **Membership.** If your club has paid memberships, you will need someone to track the memberships, sign up new members and send out renewal notices.

10. **Military Liaison.** If you have military veterans in your area, a military liaison will be a good position for another veteran to fill.

11. **Newsletter Editor and Co-Editor,** which is a good way to make sure there are people managing, tracking and developing information for the club newsletter and it's not falling on just one person.

12. **Partnership Liaison.** If your club works with other area groups, a partnership liaison can keep track of memorandums of understanding and other mutually-beneficial arrangements.

13. **Photographers.** So often overlooked but it's key to take photos of your meetings to document activities and to share them. With cell phones today, most everyone can take photos. Make a list of the photos you need and get a show of hands on who is taking photos. Get at least 2 photographers so that you increase your chances of getting all of the photos you need.

14. **Program Chair.** This person works on developing the club's monthly discussion topics and may reach out to others for hands-on demos, speakers and so forth.

15. **Refreshments.** This can start out as borrowing a coffee pot but should include at a minimum coffee and water; later add tea with honey. Nah-ah, you should not skip this, I have heard people say they will come to beginning meetings only if there is coffee. This is also where you can encourage a sense of community building by inviting people to bring food to share and nope, we don't care if its homemade or not.

16. **Security.** If meetings are in unsafe parts of town and last late into the evening, some clubs have people assigned to make sure attendees are walked safely to their cars.

17. **Special Events Coordinators.** If you have hands on demos, or an annual event of some sort like a honey tasting contest, these people are responsible for "herding the cats" around those events.
18. **Tech Support.** Identify someone who is comfortable with online platforms. Find out if it's PC- or Apple-based. There is a difference and, no, don't assume they are interchangeable.
19. **Vendor Liaison.** Someone who works with businesses having items for sale at your event.
20. **Volunteer Recruiter.** That's right, have someone designated to help you sign up volunteers. Give them a list of things that the club needs help with and let the recruiter do the outreach.
21. **Webmaster.** If you are going to have a website, you will need someone to manage it for you. Usually website content is provided to the webmaster to post.

ENGAGING BEEKEEPING HELP

Let's face it, some people attend local bee club meetings because they are looking for help. Mentors are currently hard to find and those who do can only help one or two people at a time. One alternative that has worked well for our club is our club **"buddy system,"** which we encourage at both our classes and club meetings.

If you want to start a mentoring program, it helps to have clear expectations. Here is how I define **four different beekeeping levels** and the expectations at each level.

NEWBEE

A newbee is someone who is just starting to keep bees who would like someone to help them with hands on experience, something more than talking about what the bees are doing. Most newbees want a "mentor" or someone who can provide hands on experience. I encourage them to **find a bee buddy first** and here's why.

- It's scary to open up that hive and have thousands of bees flying around you. However, the times I tried to help beginning beekeepers I found they **expected me to do the work for them.** A mentor is not someone who is going to do the beekeeping for you, this is someone who is going to be there **when YOU do it** and who may guide you on specific techniques.

- If you are just starting and want help, get up the courage to at least open a hive and get comfortable with bees flying around you. As a beginning beekeeper, you will also need to:

    a. **Learn the terminology** of beekeeping, a bee colony and bee hives.
    b. Know **basic tool use.**
    c. Have your **safety equipment in hand.**
    d. **Have extra equipment.**
    e. **Don't be afraid** to ask questions.
    f. **Listen.**

The last one, **to listen, is important** because there will be a LOT of information coming your way and it's too easy to reject a good half of it outright. A good mentor will help you build on the basics and, even though you don't understand what is being said, you may recognize later the behavior described in the hive.

BEE BUDDIES

A bee buddy is someone who is **starting when you are.** They are also preferably close to where you live so you can visit each other's bees, compare notes, share information and double your learning curve by observing and sharing what you see your bees doing.

- It's recommended that a new beekeeper start with two hives. However, if you have a bee buddy, you can each **support the other one** with each of your hives.

- Another advantage of having a bee buddy is you can **consolidate orders** to get free shipping and borrow equipment if you need something at the last minute.

Discuss your **mutual expectations** when you meet and as you are getting to know each other so you both know what to expect.

PRACTICING BEEKEEPERS

As more people show an interest in beekeeping, we need successful **practicing beekeepers** to pitch in. Practicing beekeepers are beekeepers who have successfully been keeping bees including successfully helping their colonies through winter and using the basic beekeeping skills of splitting, re-queening, making nucleus colonies and managing for pests and diseases.

Practicing beekeepers are also ones who can do demonstrations, presentations and answer questions at meetings. They don't take on individual beekeepers to mentor but can provide **invaluable information.**

MENTORS

A mentor is an experienced beekeeper who takes a less experienced beekeeper under their wing, answers questions, takes them out to work apiaries and engages the beekeeper with hands-on experience. If you can find someone close by, even better.

To fully appreciate the help of a mentor, the beginning beekeeper needs to have **some experience under their belt** so most newbies are frankly not ready for a mentor.

CERTIFIED MASTER BEEKEEPERS

Master beekeepers are beekeepers who have completed a university-sponsored beekeeping program:

- Some master beekeeping programs are **certification programs.** To qualify, a beekeeper takes a written exam and goes before a board of beekeepers to get tested about what they know. They are then "certified" and issued a certificate that they are a master beekeeper.
- Other master beekeeping programs, such as the Great Plains Master Beekeeping program out of the University of Nebraska at Lincoln, are **education programs.** Education programs guide beekeepers in learning best management practices and preparing them to be **coaches, mentors** and better beekeepers.

THE MAGIC OF NAME TAGS

Many clubs forget that for people to get to know each other it helps to **know their names.** As you start, **invest in paper name tags.**

- Encourage people to fill out their **name and hometowns.** That will provide a conversation starter as people mingle around the coffee pot.
- Having the hometown listed will also help neighbors to more **easily find each other** and follow up later on their own, maybe even develop a bee buddy.
- As your bee club gets regulars such as your oversight planning group, look into the option of getting **permanent name tags.** You can present them as a thank you at the end of the year and award them as someone takes over an ongoing club function. You can get the magnetic ones that can easily be attached to shirts and blouses for as little as $5 each from professional name tag companies.

TABLE SIGNS

Whether it's a meal during a beekeeping class or a special club event that includes a meal, consider having **table signs** to encourage those attending to get to know each other.

Names of towns. This may encourage people from the same towns to meet over a meal and possibly become bee buddies.

- **Reasons for keeping bees:** pollination, honey, bee sales, hive products. Helps beekeepers find others who are pursuing a similar beekeeping path.
- **Signs with beekeeping trivia.** Easy way to share educational information in an informal setting and give those at the table something to talk about.
- **Welcome signs.** To be friendly and inclusive. If you have kids, have them paint the signs for a real fun artistic flair.

KEEP A LIST, CHECK IT TWICE

It is so easy to get involved in something and overlook, or worse yet, forget someone who pitched in, especially in special events. Those people who do the little things are potential recruits for other duties so **keep track of who has done what** and make sure to **thank them.**

In addition, if there are people who have gone out of their way to help you, add them to your list and when the event is over, recognize them. **Hand-written notes** or, better yet, **honey jars** are a nice way to show your appreciation to someone who has given you a hand. Or two.

BEEKEEPING ETIQUETTE

Beginning beekeepers often need help with more than just advice. When practicing beekeepers provide immediately-needed supplies and equipment, new beekeepers should be reminded **to keep track, replace and or return borrowed equipment.**

Good beekeeping etiquette also extends to helping new beekeepers be **good neighbors. Remind them** in presentations and lectures that:

- **Be aware of your local laws** concerning beekeeping and follow them.
- Place your bees **away from paths** and high traffic areas. Use a fence to encourage them to fly up instead of horizontally.
- Be sensitive to neighbors who may be scared of bees. Spend time **to educate them** about what and how your bees live.
- **Follow best management practices.** Viruses and diseases in your colonies will spread to surrounding bee colonies.

HOW TO RETAIN BEE CLUB VOLUNTEERS

One of the better ways to retain volunteers is to **get to know your volunteers and what motivates them.** These may sound simple but you may be surprised at how many bee clubs I see where the leadership can't even call their volunteers by their correct first names.

- **Why are** your volunteers at your bee club, what attracted them to your group.
- Remember to be considerate of their contributions. **Listen to their suggestions;** they may have a better idea.
- Make it **fun.**

- **THANK them!**
- Sometimes people don't know how they can help so **make it clear what needs to get done.** Make up a list of duties that need to be performed; post a sign-up sheet on your website and have one at your meetings; ask for volunteers at meetings and call individuals who may be able to help.
- Ask current volunteers if they know someone **who might help** and have them recruit new volunteers.
- **Did I mention to thank them??**

VOLUNTEER TURN OVER

On the average, people **volunteer for 1-2 years** so prepare for turnover and don't take it personally if someone doesn't stick around.

- On the other hand, if someone leaves abruptly, **find out why.** It may be that someone was offended or something was frustrating enough to make them leave. The issue may be one you need to address so that it doesn't discourage other people from volunteering.
- Even if someone leaves abruptly, **make sure to thank them.** You may never know why they left so assume the best and show your gratitude for the time they did volunteer to spend. We should all hope people leave on good terms.
- Finally, **never ask someone to do something that you wouldn't be willing to do** yourself, and never ever scream at them to do what you tell them to do. Unless the place is on fire or a tornado is imminent, there is **no excuse** for having a meltdown and disrespecting people. You would be surprised to know this is more common that one might think so go into this expecting **your own best behavior.**

THE POWER OF A WRITTEN THANK YOU NOTE

As we become ever more electronically connected, the **value of handwritten notes continues on the rise.** I know several people who were successful applying for jobs because they wrote a sincere thank you note after the job interview.

Writing the notes can take time, and some thought, but the fact that you took the time to write the note and recognize someone's specific contribution, **may keep them coming back.** Contrary to some assumptions, a thank you note doesn't have to be long but it does have to be **accurate and sincere.**

SAMPLE THANK YOU NOTE

Hi, (Name), your help with (event) was greatly appreciated. Your (describe what they did) was an important reason why we succeeded so thank you for volunteering. We are a success because of volunteers like you!

Warmly/sincerely/yours in bees and beekeeping,

(signed)

CLUB VOLUNTEER JOBS CHECK LIST (IN ALPHABETICAL ORDER)

☐ Bee Wranglers
Name: _____
Start/End Dates: _____

☐ Fundraisers
Name: _____
Start/End Dates: _____

☐ Club Ambassadors
Name: _____
Start/End Dates: _____

☐ Greeters
Name: _____
Start/End Dates: _____

☐ Communications
Name: _____
Start/End Dates: _____

☐ Medical Support
Name: _____
Start/End Dates: _____

☐ Community Relations
Name: _____
Start/End Dates: _____

☐ Meeting Logistics
Name: _____
Start/End Dates: _____

BEE CLUB BASICS

☐ **Membership**
Name: _____
Start/End Dates: _____

☐ **Refreshments**
Name: _____
Start/End Dates: _____

☐ **Military Liaison**
Name: _____
Start/End Dates: _____

☐ **Security**
Name: _____
Start/End Dates: _____

☐ **Newsletter Editor and Co-Editor**
Name: _____
Start/End Dates: _____

☐ **Special Events Coordinators**
Name: _____
Start/End Dates: _____

☐ **Partnership Liaison**
Name: _____
Start/End Dates: _____

☐ **Tech Support**
Name: _____
Start/End Dates: _____

☐ **Photographer**
Name: _____
Start/End Dates: _____

☐ **Volunteer Recruiter**
Name: _____
Start/End Dates: _____

☐ **Program Chair**
Name: _____
Start/End Dates: _____

☐ **Webmaster**
Name: _____
Start/End Dates: _____

DID YOU KNOW?

- US is home to more than 4,000 native bees out of the estimated 20,000 native bees worldwide.
- Honey bees are not born knowing how to make honey. Instead, they are taught in the hive by older bees.
- Honey bees can be trained to locate buried land mines. (Not surprising if you consider honey bees easily locate hummingbird feeders!)

(Courtesy of Beepods.com)

CHAPTER 9

Monthly Bee Club Programs

"The only time I ever believed that I knew all there was to know about beekeeping was the first year I was keeping them."
— *Sue Hubbell (1935-2018)*
"A Country Year" Missouri author and beekeeper

This was one of the **most asked-for items** when I used to answer our state association email inbox. Here are a few suggestions on how to get started developing monthly bee club programs.

- **Tap your local experienced beekeepers.** Even if they don't attend your bee club meetings, they should be able to give you an outline of what needs to be done and discussed month to month. And yes, this can vary from one area to the next.

- If you don't know the best months to cover particular topics, **brain storm a list of topics** and people you know who may be able to talk about a particular topic. Sometimes the speakers can help you better organize a program calendar based on their local expertise.

*Include a **club program every month** on a pertinent current beekeeping topic and tap your existing club members for presentations. Bee headbands, although a personal favorite, are purely optional!*

- **Beware of pulling any program off an online platform,** not all techniques are appropriate for your particular area. I tell our beekeeping students don't trust a beekeeper in a new suit or a gardener with clean fingernails.
- **Encourage club attendees to bring items to "show and tell."** It can be photos, a frame, maybe something they cooked with honey – some of the more interesting discussions we've had at our bee club meetings came from people who had a story to tell. **Create an environment where people are comfortable sharing.**

BEE CLUB MEETING POSSIBLE TOPICS

There are several ways you can organize your bee club meetings around discussion topics appropriate to your area. If you are a beekeeper, **make a list** of the things you do and build from there. Tap other beekeepers and have them review and update your list.

Here is a **basic annual calendar of monthly program topics** you can customize for your area. Make sure to include a time to discuss *Varroa* management options and planting forage.

JANUARY

- Welcome, happy new year
- Winter feeding
- Pollen feeding
- Understanding nectar
- Making wax frames and woodenware

FEBRUARY

- Welcome, bees are nature's matchmakers!
- Hive Repairs
- Spring build-up
- *Varroa* management plan
- Planting for pollinators

MARCH

- Hello spring!
- How are your bees?
- Preparing for nectar flow
- Understanding pollen
- Spring Inspections
- Locating Hives
- *Varroa* management

APRIL

- Welcome, do I know you?
- Swarm monitoring
- Spring nectar flow Projections
- How to start smoker
- Package installation
- Nuc care tips
- Drone removal for *Varroa* management

MAY

- Welcome, happy Mother's Day
- How to mark queen (using drones)
- Catching swarms
- Feeding Nucs
- May 20 World Bee Day
- *Varroa* management

JUNE

- Hi there, happy Father's Day
- End of nectar flow
- Honey Production Estimates
- Feeding Nucs
- Making Splits
- *Varroa* management

JULY

- Hi, welcome, here's to Fourth of July!
- Honey extracting
- Oxalic acid application demonstration
- Robbing
- *Varroa* management

AUGUST

- Hi, warm enough?
- The dearth and lack of forage
- *Varroa* mite treatment options
- Signs of Robbing

SEPTEMBER

- Hello, fall
- Fall nectar flow
- Reducing Hives
- Supplemental winter feeding
- Planting for pollinators
- *Varroa* management

OCTOBER

- Welcome, Trick or treat
- Hive repairs
- How to store frames and equipment
- Winter Preparations
- *Varroa* management

NOVEMBER

- Happy Thanksgiving
- Winter feeding
- What worked well
- *Varroa* management Oxalic Acid application
- Bee ordering options

DECEMBER

- Merry Christmas and Happy New Year
- Goals for next year
- White Elephant Gift Exchange

*When making presentations, **include items that will help you make your point**. I carry a 1-pound honey bottle (center) to drive home that it takes the dehydrated flower nectar of 2 million blossoms to make the honey in that bottle. And yes, I do love wearing the bee headband in my planting for pollinators presentation. It reminds the audience that we are looking at a garden from a bee's perspective, another item that helps emphasize the point of the lecture.*

FREQUENTLY-ASKED QUESTIONS ABOUT FINDING SPEAKERS

A. **Where do we find speakers?**

- **Who showed up** to your very first meetings, anyone with beekeeping experience?
- Look at who your local service clubs, chambers of commerce and other clubs have tapped. They usually have **speakers lists** on their websites.
- Contact your **local university Extension offices** and find out what extension specialists they have on staff. Extension staff members have yearly quotas of people they should be meeting to share their expertise.
- Contact a nearby **community college or university** for their specialties and available speakers.
- Check the **state beekeeping association website** for the closest bee club to where you are. **Ask for suggestions** on who they know may be able to speak to your group and on what topics.

B. **What if the speaker doesn't agree with your views?**

- Keep **politics and religion at home.** This is a beekeeping club.
- If you're not sure of what the speaker is saying, **ask for clarification.**
- Check the **speaker's advice against suggested best management practices** and get a discussion going about different recommendations and why.
- There are some beekeepers who have book knowledge but little experience. If you need to choose, **opt for what the experienced beekeepers** are saying.
- Don't ask him/her only how they do something, ask them **what they learned when something went wrong** as well.

C. **Do we pay the speaker?**

- Ask **what the speaker wants for compensation** when you invite them to speak to your club. Local speakers usually don't ask for mileage.

- If someone is travelling any distance, it's good practice to **reimburse them at least** for gas.
- If you can get donations, **provide the speaker with a jar of honey** or other bee hive product as a thank you at the meeting.
- **Follow up** with a written thank you note.

D. What if the speaker doesn't show up?

Have a **couple of program topics ready** that would work year around. Some suggestions:

- Do a round robin and discuss **why each of you** is keeping bees.
- What have **you learned so far** in beekeeping that surprised you and why?
- Ask people **how their bees are doing.**

BEE MATH

"Bee Math" is knowing how long things should take to help beekeepers predict where colony developments are going and/or where things have been. Some experienced beekeepers will automatically start explaining colony developments assuming others know possible timelines, such as how long it should take for a virgin queen to start to lay (2-4 weeks depending on weather) or how many weeks before a queenless colony may have laying workers (3 weeks or more).

When having club discussions, remember to **include some of the "bee math"** basics to help bring beginning beekeepers along.

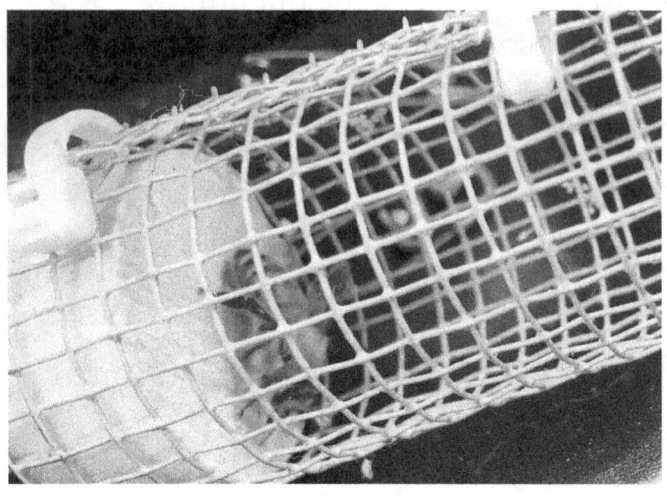

*This is a **homemade queen cage.** How long does it take for the queen to eclose? How long should you keep a queen bee caged? How long may it take for her to mate and return to the home hive and start to lay? Those numbers are all part of "bee math."*

BEE CLUB MONTHLY MEETINGS TOPICS FOR YEAR

MONTH	TOPIC	SPEAKER	NOTES	EQUIPMENT/ SUPPLIES NEEDED
January	• How to winter feed • Planting for Pollinators • Making wax frames			
February	• Pollen feeding • Repairing frames/painting • Pros and cons of buying • Beginning beekeeping kits • Winter Spring Turnover			
March	• Signs of Swarm preparation • Catching swarms • Package Installation • Spring inspections			

April	• Upcoming nectar flow • How to start smoker • Raising queens			
May	• How to mark queen • Sugar water feeding • *Varroa* powdered sugar roll • *Varroa* alcohol wash • Planting for pollinators • May 20 World Bee Day			
June	• How to raise queens • Swarm prevention • Monitoring colony growth			
July	• End of nectar flow • Signs of robbing • *Varroa* management options			
August	• How to winterize hives • Oxalic acid vapor and dribble • How to make sugar board • Honey extracting			

September	• Winter bees • Winterizing hives • Fall planting			
October	• Annual honey taste contest • How to clean smoker • Winter reading			
November	• Bee ordering options • Pros and cons of packages • Winter feeding			
December	• Celebrate the year			
January				
Notes:				

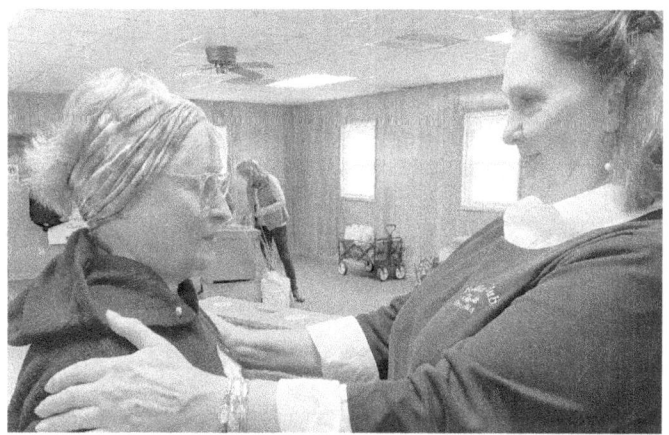

Celebrate accomplishments. Carolyn Humburg, left, from Cuba, Mo. getting her "beekeeper" pin after successfully helping her first bees through winter. (Photo courtesy Sharon Contini)

Your Notes

_____

_____

_____

_____

_____

_____

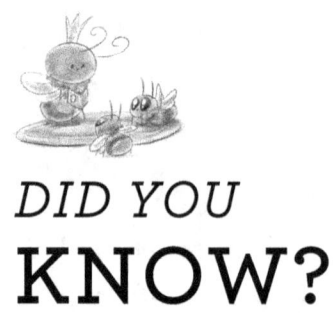

DID YOU KNOW?

- Due to the rise in popularity of urban beekeeping, it is estimated that honey bees outnumber the residents of London 30-1 in the summer months.

- In 1984, honey bees on a space shuttle constructed a honeycomb in zero gravity.

- Every bee species performs their communication dances differently.

(Courtesy of Beepods.com)

CHAPTER 10

Special Bee Club Events

"There is no such thing as too many honey bees."
— *David Draker*
My bee buddy and Rolla Bee Club co-founder

It's a bit of a mystery to me how bee clubs can talk about beekeeping without, say – honey bees. I do understand it can be challenging to get access to them but with today's technology, a video of a working hive or a series of printed photos can be just a click, and a printer, away.

When I first started keeping honey bees in 2010, I must have spent my first year attending club meetings in a total fog because of the new "language" I had to learn. Then when I questioned established practices, such as "having" to kill my queens every year, there was no explanation of my options, just a peremptory "must do."

The bottom line is make as many opportunities available as possible to **show people** beekeeping, from classes to apiary visits. Also encourage attendees to bring in examples of what is happening in their apiaries. Discussions will be better, and more accurate, **if everyone can see** what is actually happening.

*Special events can be practical such as lending a helping hand to extract honey. Just remember **not to knock open the honey gate** or you'll have slippery honey all over the place. Now ask me how I know. No, not me but maybe, oh, let's say someone like perhaps my bee buddy?*

SPECIAL BEE CLUB EVENT IDEAS

Beekeeping club discussions should be fun so here are some suggestions, in alphabetical order, on **how to add value, and sometimes funds,** to your bee club and bee club meetings.

ARTS AND CRAFTS CONTESTS

If you have beekeepers in your club and/or area that produce hive products, consider sponsoring an arts and crafts contests for hive products. The exposure will help beekeepers raise awareness about the products they make and the contest gives the club an opportunity to **showcase hive products:**

- Handmade soaps
- Lip balms
- Candles
- Creamed and comb honey
- Bee – related paintings
- **What other things** can you think of for an arts and crafts contest?

BAKE SALES

If you have active supporters who are willing to make baked items to sell in order to raise funds, lucky you. This is a **delicious way to raise funds** and requires quick planning.

- Get volunteers to offer what they will bake.
- Have someone who can price the items fairly.
- Include a list of ingredients for those who have allergies and food sensitivities.
- Package for easy viewing and protection during transportation.
- Plan far enough ahead so that you can share the bake sale information to generate interested customers.
- **Thank those who contribute.**

BAKING CONTESTS

Better yet, make it a **baking contest** with prizes to the winners. That will get people involved in sampling and voting, and provide the bakers with recognition for their delicious work.

Remember to **thank those** who make contributions and who help with the contests.

BEE BUDDIES AND MENTORS

When I hold classes, I encourage students to meet other students from their communities and establish themselves as **"bee buddies."** That way they have someone with whom they can share experiences, borrow equipment and check each other's hives. The "bee buddy" program has worked well for us in an area that doesn't have experienced beekeepers willing to invest time in mentoring new beekeepers. We introduce students in classes, then encourage everyone to wear name tags with their name and home town at meetings to facilitate introductions.

Mentors are much more difficult to find. Sometimes a mentorship relationship can develop from a club meeting but it is something that takes time to develop.

BEE CLUB NUCLEUS AND QUEEN BEE SALES

Some bee clubs raise funds through the sales of spring nucleus (nuc) colonies and queen bees. Although this can be a good fundraiser, it requires a **cadre of volunteers** to make it possible, from finding people interested in picking up nucs and queens, usually from bee providers in other states, to volunteers who help with the coordinated pick up.

This is not an activity I would recommend for a beginning bee club.

Purchasing queen bees, on the other hand, is a much easier option.

- Gather the **names and queen bee quantities** each person needs.
- You may need to limit the number of queen bees per person to make sure everyone gets at least a few queens.
- Have everyone **pre-pay for the queens** to ensure the costs are covered.
- Schedule a **pick up day** for everyone to stop by and get their queen bees.

*When setting up meetings or classes, **do a dry run**. This is one of our beginning beekeeping classes set up the day prior to the class. My bee buddy David, who shares class coaching with me, is already thinking about how to re-organize this set up to accommodate for COVID-related safety precautions.*

BEEKEEPING CLASSES

Some bee clubs raise funds by holding yearly introduction to beekeeping, beginning beekeeping and special skills classes such as queen-rearing. These classes will also **take time and a cadre of experienced beekeepers** to plan and hold the classes.

- One option is to **ask nearby club beekeepers** to come in and teach the classes or coordinate for your club members to participate in an upcoming class. The best time to plan them and ask for help is during the winter, when honey bees are not keeping beekeepers busy.
- If you decide to hold a class yourself, **divide the sections** so that several people help, that way the burden of the class doesn't fall on just one person. And we call ourselves coaches, the bees are the teachers.

Here is a **sample beginning beekeeping class outline** providing the basics for new beekeepers focused on helping their honey bees only through their first winter.

*Plan for signs to easily guide people to your class location. You can get them printed or hand-letter them yourself as long as they are **big enough letters** to be seen from a distance and from a nearby road.*

(SAMPLE) BEGINNING BEEKEEPING CLASS AGENDA

9 a.m. – 9:15 a.m.	Welcome/intros
9:15 a.m. – 10:15 am	Why Do You Want to Keep Bees?
	What Is Pollination
	History of Beekeeping
	Bee Biology
10:15 a.m. – 10:30 a.m.	*Break*
10:30 a.m. – 11:30 a.m.	How to Get Bees
	Cost of Beekeeping
	Hive Options
	Starting Equipment
	Parts of a Hive
11:30 a.m. – 12:30 p.m.	*Lunch*
12:30 p.m. – 1:30 p.m.	Make Your Own Hives
1:30 p.m. – 1:45 p.m.	How to Install Packages
1:45 p.m.– 2:45 p.m.	*Break*
	Pests and Diseases
	How to Inspect Hives
2:45 p.m.– 3 p.m.	Beekeeper's Yearly Task Calendar
3 p.m. – 3:45 p.m.	*Break*
3:45 p.m. – 4 p.m.	Questions and Answers
	Bee Buddies & Mentoring
	Class survey
	Wrap Up

BEEKEEPING CLASS SURVEY

Regardless of what classes you hold and/or sponsor, make sure to set up a way to **gauge how well you are doing.** Distributing a class survey is a helpful way to get feedback in a non-threatening way.

A class survey is also a handy method to collect ideas for other classes and related activities.

(Sample) Beekeeping Class Survey

Beginning Beekeeping Class Survey Date:_____

What did you think of the class? Please place a mark in the box that best reflects your answers and add comments for more details so we can make appropriate adjustments. Thank you!

QUESTIONS	5 GREAT	4 GOOD	3 OK	2 FAIR	1 POOR	COMMENTS
Did the class meet your expectations?						
Did you like the room?						
How were class materials?						
How could this class have been better?						
What other class topics would you be interested in?						
Any other comments?						

Your Name	Email	Phone Number	Hometown

BEEKEEPING EQUIPMENT SALES

Some bee clubs offer a **once-a-year beekeeping equipment sale** where beekeepers can bring in extra equipment and woodenware. This can be managed with a percentage of sales going to the bee club planning the sale and requires extra display and storage space in case of rain. If the bee club is located in a larger urban area, this could also be run as an auction.

BOOK SALES

- Another service a bee club can provide to meeting attendees is to have **books for sale.**
- Start by limiting book sales to **books offered in classes.**
- **Price them simply** such as in $10 and $20 book boxes so people can easily see pricing and to keep making change easy.

Shop for used beekeeping books online and gardening books at your local thrift stores, both books will be of interest to beekeepers.

GARDEN VISITS

Another good field trip is to **meet at someone's garden** and discuss what plants to plant in your USDA Hardiness zone. If it is a garden with hives, even better.

Remind everyone to take **protective equipment** and **follow safety precautions** on site.

Remember to **thank the gardener** who invited you; a jar of honey will always be welcome.

GIFT CERTIFICATES

One of the ways a beginning bee club can increase community awareness is by offering **gift certificates.**

The most popular time for these is **over December holidays.**

They also make excellent **Mother's Day** and **Father's Day** gifts.

(Sample) Beekeeping Class Gift Certificate

(Name of club/website)

Date_____

This gift certificate entitles _____

to a Beginning and/or Second Year beekeeping class at _____
in (date)_____.

Beginning classes (list dates)

To register, email (add email) and call (phone number)

_____

Certificate No. _____

(Signed) Club Officer

_____

Print on cardboard stock and place in an envelope.

Keep track of the numbers sold by numbering them and listing who bought them.

*Whenever talking about honey, and/or tasting honey, **include flowers** in your discussion: current blooming plants, ask who can identify the flowers, discuss how different honeys will look, and taste differently based on what flowers the bees have visited. This is a bouquet of fall blooming flowers from my garden; I left a little folded card on the honey tasting table identifying the flowers. Can you? Yellow and burgundy Chrysanthemums, New England Asters, Dark pink Vinca and blooming Spearmint.*

HOLIDAY DINNERS

To build a sense of community, it is nice to **host an annual dinner**, picnic or periodic potluck where spouses can get to meet other bee club members. If you are going to host a dinner, make sure it is held in a location that can accommodate all regular club attendees and family members, not just a small group of club insiders.

If you can't find a big enough location, it is best to plan something at a bee club meeting and not restrict those who can attend the event. I have seen bee clubs host similar events but restrict attendance, which ended up in them loosing members. Everyone has a right to include whoever they wish but if you want to be welcoming, plan events so that **everyone who is interested** can participate.

HONEY TASTING CONTESTS

Speaking of talking about flowers, hosting a honey tasting contest can get family members and friends involved and exposed to bee club meetings. After all, who would pass up tasting a variety of honeys?

You can use the honey tasting contest **for several reasons:**

- As an opportunity to talk about the **connection between bees and flowers;**
- **As a fundraiser.** A number of regional and national groups raise funds by hosting honey contests and then selling the contributions.
- If you follow State Fair Honey judging rules, as a **first step** to entering local honey in a State Fair Honey contest.

To host a honey-tasting contest, you need to let bee club attendees know **by late spring** so they can start planning for the contest. Rolla Bee Club holds their contest in October but you can set it up whenever it best fits your program schedule.

- The simplest way to get entries is to specify **unmarked glass jars** with the name of the person on the glass jar bottom who is entering the honey. The idea is to not have a way to identify the beekeeper.
- Entries for **established contests** such as the Missouri State Fair Honey Contest and Heartland Apicultural Society Honey contest specify the type and size of jars, etc. Check associated contest websites for honey contest rules. Then follow them.

You will need **a way to number the jars;** we use pieces of paper with numbers on them in front of jars.

For taste testing, **toothpicks** and containers to hold **new and used toothpicks.** Tasters take a new toothpick, dip it in the honey, roll it to get honey on the toothpick and taste; then discard that toothpick and select another one.

To vote, we give participants three plastic poker chips each. They then place the chips in front of the honey jar they like best and the honey with the highest number of chips wins.

We have first, second and third place ribbons attached to different-sized wood honey dippers and post photos of the winners on our club website and the state association newsletter and social media sites.

For an **easy special category,** try a **black jar honey contest.** Jars of honey are painted black so no one can see the honey color when it is being taste-tested. Mark the bottom of the jar with the beekeeper's name.

We have had beekeepers on their own donate their winning honey as a **club giveaway.** Others sell their winning honey as a **fundraiser.**

MILITARY VETERAN SUPPORT PROGRAMS

There are a number of military veteran support programs from locally-sponsored ones to ones national in scope. The University of Michigan, in cooperation with several other Midwest University partners, sponsors a **free beginning beekeeping program nationwide for military veterans.** Combining extensive online courses with monthly open apiary hands-on events, the program is designed to help military veterans safely transition to civilian life and potentially raise bees as a business venture.

The Heroes to Hives program, with their first chapter in Missouri, is open to military veterans and their immediate family members. Online classes start March 1. Beginning beekeepers are encouraged to take the classes their first year and start keeping bees during their second year. This program **depends on local clubs** to welcome and support this new influx of beekeepers. As of this writing, the program is expanding nationwide, providing local bee clubs and state associations with the potential of new members.

https://bit.ly/HeroesHives

Full disclosure here. I am the military advisor to Missouri's Heroes to Hives Chapter, the first licensed Heroes to Hives Chapter in the country. I'm not paid. I do provide program recommendations. Go Navy.

MISSOURI'S UNIQUE MASTER POLLINATOR STEWARD PROGRAM

Spring of 2019, University of Missouri's College of Natural Resources launched a 5-class program designed to teach Missouri residents about the value of pollinators, how they contribute to our food chain and what we can do to help them and our interdependent ecosystems. The award-winning Missouri Master Pollinator Steward Program is the **first program in the country** to work through partners such as master gardeners, master naturalists and bee clubs to educate the public. The nationally-award winning program was designed to engage those people who have an interest in bees but don't want to keep them.

As one of the contributing writers and members of the Steering Committee, we designed the program to connect these classes with local bee clubs by splitting class revenue with local bee club sponsors.

For more information, visit https://bit.ly/EDU-Steward.

Open apiaries are a good opportunity to get hands on experience and try out equipment such as this motorized hive lifter at Central Missouri State University's Warrensburg Open Apiary supporting Missouri's Heroes to Hives Chapter. The program provides free first year online and hands on beekeeping lessons to military veterans and their immediate families.

OPEN (TEACHING) APIARIES

One of the more exciting benefits of our local club is that it is located close to a private apiary we can visit. If you have ever seen a potential beekeeper first experience having a bee land on a gloved finger, you know in that instant **that's when the connection** is made.

Some clubs are big enough to have working apiaries, also referred to as open apiaries. These locations have bees where club members can meet with an experienced beekeeper for hands on experience. Some also have a speaker; others just focus on a discussion at the hives.

- Signed waivers inform participants to be careful but **do not eliminate** the property owner's responsibility if something goes wrong. If you **don't have liability insurance**, the private landowner takes on the liability when inviting people onto his/her property.
- To protect the bee club, **get insurance coverage** that will provide liability for off club site events. Your local farm bureau and agriculture-related insurance companies often are the sources of reasonably-priced insurance.
- The other must have for apiary visits is that attendees have to **wear protective equipment, no exceptions**.
- A **safety briefing** before approaching the hives is also a good idea, reviewing what to do if someone is stung, where to go if someone falls and so forth.

PHOTOGRAPHY CONTESTS

Of all contests this may be the **easiest one to plan and manage.** Set up requirements, such as acceptable photo sizes, what will and won't be allowed, submission deadline and ask a club photographer to review the entries. Great opportunity for beekeepers to share their photos and provide opportunities for further discussion.

Some groups get local sponsors to fund monetary awards.

Ask entrants for permission to share their photos. This can be a source of good photography for your website, flyers and other information products.

SWARM LISTS

Can you think of anything that excites a beekeeper more than just the thought of **catching a swarm?** It's also a great way to connect beekeepers with their local communities since the majority of people want to help "save bees." One way your bee club can help is to **offer a swarm-catching list** that is updated yearly so that it is current. The list should have names, the range they will cover as well as a cell phone number.

The swarm list can be posted on your website, shared through emails and also offered to your local police, fire department and pest control operators so they have the information handy during swarm season.

It is helpful to **list the questions to ask** when someone reports a swarm:

1. Are you sure they are honey bees? Text a photo.
2. How far off the ground are they?
3. Are they easily accessible?
4. Are you the property owner?
5. Settle any costs associated with swarm catching. For example, if a wall has to be removed that will require contacting a contractor unless you are one and want to provide that additional service.

In a couple of instances, property owners tried to charge for the honey bees so think through how you want to handle that development.

In another instance, I heard a property owner tried to sue a nearby beekeeper alleging a swarm came from his apiary.

In most cases, though, people are **helpful and curious** about the process.

- Plan on **taking time to answer questions** about honey bee swarms, it's a great opportunity to educate the public.
- **Don't make commitments** about providing honey since most swarms don't make it through their first winter. You don't want to set up expectations you can't easily keep.

Before listing people, it is a good idea to go over some of the basics of responding to a swarm call including how to keep bystanders safe and making sure those posted have experience catching swarms.

Please **include a disclaimer** that the names are offered for information only, the actions of the beekeepers are their own.

PLANTING FOR POLLINATORS

Tap your local master gardeners for a class or two on planting for pollinators. Master gardeners and related groups are trained to share information on a variety of topics and usually have a speaker's bureau with lecturers that cover a variety of topics.

When talking about planting for pollinators, people usually want a list of plants. Before even thinking about what to plant, find out **what kind of soil they have.** Most University extension offices offer a soil test that will provide specific soil information and what to do to amend it. Sponsor getting soil collected to get a soil test and review the findings so beekeepers understand how to use the soil test information. Most soil tests cost $15-$25.

I would be remiss if I didn't include this **quick guide** on how to **help bees with better forage:**

- Don't use pesticides, insecticides, herbicides – nerve-affecting chemicals and certainly don't mix any of these.
- Plant a variety of native plants in **large, single species clumps.**
- **Provide blooming flowers all season.** Not sure what to plant? Plant native trees and shrubs, locate those that provide nectar and pollen, they are usually highlighted in catalogs.
- **Fruit trees** are an excellent source of bee food when they are blooming, especially the stone fruit trees such as apricots, cherry, peach, plums.
- Most states have lists of the **leading nectar and pollen sources** for their area and yes, they will be different.
- Check your community's noxious weed ordinances first as your community may have outdated "weeds" on their list. Beekeepers can help to educate their city leaders to encourage pollinator support plantings and remove the **misnomer of "noxious weeds."**
- If you do nothing else to help feed your bees, compost. **Composting** is a free and easy way to "feed" the microorganisms in soil that keep plants, and therefore pollinators like bees, healthy.

WHITE ELEPHANT EXCHANGES

Over the holidays, sponsor a white elephant exchange where participants **bring an item in a bag or gift-wrapped to exchange.**

- Participants pull numbers out of a box and proceed to **pick out a package** to open based on the number they selected.
- To keep the exchange moving, **allow one steal** by the next person in line.
- Then the person who lost the item **goes back to the table** and selects another bag to open.
- Fun way **to share items** no longer being used and getting to see new equipment.
- **Limit the steal to one time** or this event will continue for days!

*Include one good item in the elephant exchange to **motivate people** to participate such as honey signs.*

SAMPLE MONTHLY BEE CLUB TOPICS CALENDAR

I have each month listed separately so these can be **distributed among volunteers** who may be interested in planning a particular month's events.

- Also marked are **suggested topics** for everyone to discuss.
- These are only starting points; feel free **to add or substitute** topics that better fit your beekeeping community's schedule and needs.
- If you don't like the suggested topics, just make sure to include a place where **people can discuss what is happening with their bees.**

BEE CLUB MONTHLY TOPICS CALENDAR: JANUARY				
Check off	Topic	Speaker	Need	Notes
	• Welcome • New Year's Resolutions	All		
	Winter feeding			
	February Pollen feeding			
	Making wax frames and woodenware			
	Other:			

SPECIAL BEE CLUB EVENTS

BEE CLUB MONTHLY TOPICS CALENDAR: FEBRUARY

Check Off	Topic	Speaker	Need	Notes
	• Welcome • Bees as Nature's Matchmakers			
	• Late winter • Feeding; how are bees so far	All		
	Planting For Pollinators			
	What are you planting for your bees?	All		
	Understanding Pollen			
	Hive Repairs			
	Spring Build up			
	Other:			

©2022 CHARLOTTE EKKER WIGGINS

BEE CLUB MONTHLY TOPICS CALENDAR: MARCH

Check Off	Topic	Speaker	Need	Notes
	Welcome Spring			
	How are your bees?	All		
	Preparing for the Nectar Flow			
	Varroa Management plan			
	Spring Inspections			
	Locating Hives			
	Other:			

BEE CLUB MONTHLY TOPICS CALENDAR: APRIL

Check Off	Topic	Speaker	Need	Notes
	• Welcome • Swarm Monitoring	All		
	Spring Nectar Flow Projections			
	How to Re-queen			
	Drone removal for *Varroa* management			
	Nuc Care Tips			
	Package Installation			
	How to Manage Smoker			
	Other:			

BEE CLUB MONTHLY TOPICS CALENDAR: MAY

Check Off	Topic	Speaker	Need	Notes
	• Welcome • Happy Mother's Day • May 20 World Bee Day			
	Managing Nectar Flow			
	Marking queens (with Drones)	All		
	Catching Swarms			
	Feeding Nucs			
	Other:			

SPECIAL BEE CLUB EVENTS

BEE CLUB MONTHLY TOPICS CALENDAR: JUNE

Check Off	Topic	Speaker	Need	Notes
	• Welcome • Happy Father's Day			
	End of Nectar Flow			
	Making Splits			
	Honey Production Estimates	All		
	Feeding Nucs			
	Varroa Management			
	Other:			

BEE CLUB MONTHLY TOPICS CALENDAR: JULY

Check Off	Topic	Speaker	Need	Notes
	• Welcome • Happy 4th!			
	Honey Extracting	All		
	Varroa Management			
	Supplemental Feeding			
	Winter Prep			
	Other:			

SPECIAL BEE CLUB EVENTS

BEE CLUB MONTHLY TOPICS CALENDAR: AUGUST				
Check Off	Topic	Speaker	Need	Notes
	• Welcome • Back to School			
	Impacts of Dearth	All		
	Fall Nectar Flow and Feeding			
	Signs of Robbing			
	Varroa Management			
	Other:			

BEE CLUB MONTHLY TOPICS CALENDAR: SEPTEMBER

Check Off	Topic	Speaker	Need	Notes
	Welcome Fall			
	Fall Nectar Flow	All		
	Planting For Pollinators			
	Varroa Management			
	Supplemental Winter Feeding			
	Other:			

BEE CLUB MONTHLY TOPICS CALENDAR: OCTOBER

Check Off	Topic	Speaker	Need	Notes
	• Welcome • Trick or Treat			
	Hive Repairs			
	How to Store Frames and Equipment			
	Winter Prep	All		
	Other:			

BEE CLUB MONTHLY TOPICS CALENDAR: NOVEMBER

Check Off	Topic	Speaker	Need	Notes
	• Welcome • Happy Thanksgiving			
	Winter Feeding			
	What worked well this past year	All		
	Varroa management: Oxalic Acid			
	Ordering Bees			
	Other:			

TELLING PEOPLE ABOUT YOUR MEETINGS

1. Meeting notices **include the basics:**

   - **Who:** name of your club
   - **What:** monthly, special meeting, special event
   - **When:** date, and include day, month and year
   - **Where:** location with a specific address (checked against GPS)
   - **Why:** reason event taking place; include speaker and topic, describe event (extracting demo)
   - **With Whom:** who is welcome
   - **Cost:** mention if there is a cost associated
   - **Website and/or Facebook page:** list these sites for more information
   - **Point of contact:** name, email, phone number if someone is coordinating specifics.

2. Make sure the meeting notice information is **consistent with other posted and shared information.** If not, make them consistent to reduce confusion.

3. **Keep a list** of where you post it in case **you need to change it** later. Reasons to change may include cancellations and postponements due to weather, scheduling conflicts, change of planned activities.

SAMPLE BEE CLUB MEETING NOTICES

This is how information can be pulled together for a community calendar notice:

1. The Eldon Bee Club will meet Saturday, January 1, 2019 at the Community Center from 2 – 4 p.m. Everyone is welcome. For more details, email ***bees@gmail.com and call (000) 000-0000.

Or

The Eldon Bee Club will meet Saturday, January 1, 2019 at the Community Center from 2-4 p.m. The agenda includes how to winter feed bees. Volunteers are welcome to discuss fundraising ideas. No dues. (Or donations appreciated) Refreshments will be available. For further information, visit eldonbeeclub.com, email ***bees@gmail.com and call (000) 000-0000.

Your Notes

_____

_____

_____

_____

_____

_____

DID YOU KNOW?

- In the Hittite Empire (1600 BCE), which is modern day Turkey and Syria, a swarm's value was equal to that of one sheep.

- A single ounce of honey could fuel a honey bee's flight all the way around the world.

- Honey bees are being used to study dementia. When a honey bee takes on a new job usually done by a younger bee, its brain stops aging.

(Courtesy of Beepods.com)

CHAPTER 11

Getting the Word Out

Who said "If the bee disappeared off the face of the earth, man would only have four years left to live." Was it:

A. Rachel Carson   B. Albert Einstein

C. Maurice Maeterlinck   D. Reverend Langstroth

The answer to the question is somewhere later in this chapter.

This is such an important element to making your meetings successful but it may also be the most unappreciated part of meeting management; **how to share information** about your meetings and upcoming planned club activities.

ESTABLISH AN EMAIL LIST

Regardless of your organizational structure, a **contact email list** is essential for running your bee club.

- **Have a sign-up sheet** available at every meeting and have someone responsible for collecting emails. It is a good opportunity to tap early arrivals to help and greet others as they come in.

Share information with club members. **Request free magazine copies** *from publishers and brochures from your state association. Mark them as "free" to keep them separate from items you are selling. Encourage other free contributions such as egg cartons to recycle and/or egg cartons with local eggs, hint, hint.*

- Once you have an email list, **set up a mailing list** in an email management platform. Those usually offer a direct email sign-up that will make managing the email list much easier than struggling to read people's hand-writing.
- If you are sending emails, **send your emails blind copy** so you are protecting those who shared their emails with you.

TAKE LOTS OF PHOTOS

We are a **visual society.** Pictures are better than words.

- Have **at least 2 people** who are willing to take photos to document initial meetings, speakers and other activities. These will come in handy when you start a website and share information on posters and other outlets.
- If there are under age attendees, get a **signed release form from the parent.** If the parent says they don't want the minor's photo used, delete the photo. Don't assume someone will remember later or check the consent forms. It is best to entirely remove photos of minors.
- Also make sure people in photos are wearing the **proper safety equipment** for the situation. Don't reward unsafe practices by using their photos unless it is for an example of what not to do.
- Photos online are there forever so **carefully select photos** before you post!

HOW BEST TO STAY IN TOUCH

Every group of people may have their own unique combination of how to share information. One of the clubs I used to attend posted their meetings and associated information only on a bulletin board outside the monthly meeting room. Another one liked to post flyers on bathroom stalls. The bottom line is **ask how your beginning group** wants to share information and do it.

Start with sharing information with your club members **at your meetings:**

- Offer free information such as association brochures.
- Magazines.
- Handout copies.

Often people assume that the Internet is the way to share information but in rural parts of the US, there are still pockets where the Internet is not accessible. You may need to have a **backup way** to provide those members with information.

Some beekeepers do not use email services so may need a phone call or other way to be contacted. Options include **texting** and having **another person in the bee club** responsible for sharing information with this person.

The easiest way to share information is to do it at **a bee club meeting.** That requires the club planning team to be organized and have event information planned ahead of time.

- Sign-up sheets
- Hand outs
- Event flyer copies (8.5x 11 size for bulletin boards)
- Poster board with information

WHAT INFORMATION TO SHARE

For whatever event including bee club meetings, you will need:
- **Who** (your group)
- **What** (meeting, having coffee – what are you doing?)
- **Where** (location including an address)
- **When** (time)
- **Why** (purpose for getting together)
- **How Much** (whether there is a fee or its free)
- ***Contact information** (name, email, phone number)

*Sort out beforehand who will be **the group contact person** and make sure they have all pertinent info. If you change a meeting date, let them know and so forth.

Also **keep track** of where you share the information in case you need to update it.

So you have a club email list and someone comes along and asks you for a copy. Do you give it to them?

GUARD YOUR BEE CLUB EMAIL LIST

Your email list will be your club's most important asset so **manage it carefully** and well.

- Use the email list for **only the express intended purpose.**
- **Do not share**, sell or otherwise give anyone else access to your email list.
- If you want to change the initial expressed purpose, first ask the names on the email if that's ok and **respect their decision.**

If someone wants to reach your members, give your club the information on how they can be added, **do not provide your list to anyone.**

BEE CLUB NEWSLETTER

It's easy to get over-extended when developing a newsletter so **set goals** before you get started and have co-editors so they can share the load.

- A bee club newsletter should have **the basics** that participating beekeepers would like to have: upcoming meeting dates, helpful resources and who to contact for help.
- Other helpful information is to follow up with **information associated with club discussions** such as recipes for sugar syrup, small hive beetle lures and pollen substitute.
- To best manage a club newsletter, have **written guidelines** for whoever is collecting the information as the editor.

As you become more proficient with your newsletter and the platform you are using, you can also **offer to sell space** in the newsletter for advertising, which will provide your bee club with an extra revenue source.

NEWSLETTER IDEAS

Newsletters can be as simple as a nice email that you blind copy to protect the privacy of people who shared their emails with you to something more elaborate.

The following are **typical newsletter subjects:**

- Topics and speakers scheduled for next meeting
- Upcoming fund-raising events
- Description of volunteer opportunities
- Description of the mission of your club
- Current and upcoming beekeeping duties
- Helpful links
- Recipes
- Sign up to club email list
- New developments in scientific research
- News from your corporate supporters

BEE CLUB WEBSITE

In our online world, a club website makes it easier for people to locate basic meeting information and know who to contact.

There are some simple website hosting platforms that charge $8/month and more extensive website hosting options. These established website platforms **keep the sites secure** and provide **easy to use** website design software. **Start simple;** then when you outgrow your web host, upgrade to support your expanding club needs.

What to include on your website? Collect and share the **basic information** someone would like to know about the club:

- Who you are
- Meeting dates
- What you're planning for upcoming meetings
- Special events such as classes, speakers
- Contact email

The website is your **depository for information, your library.** Now you need to connect existing and potential club attendees with the posted information.

DO'S AND DON'TS OF SOCIAL MEDIA

Every day there seems to be a new social media platform to share information. Use social media **only if that's where your potential club members can be found.** To effectively use social media, it takes a lot of time and consistent effort to do it well.

Social media is **NOT a substitute** for telling people at your club meetings, emailing them and including in a newsletter. If you are **limited on time, focus on these three.** If, however, you are in an area where your beekeepers like to use it, in general, keep these **basic principles** in mind:

- Is it **true?**
- Is it **kind?**
- Is it **necessary?**

Remember these posts are permanent so **think carefully** before posting.

When using social media, don't:

- Believe everything you read. **Check sources!**
- Repeat negative statements.
- Argue online with something posted.
- Tag people without asking permission first.
- Share very personal information.
- Post photos you don't want someone else to use.
- Use profanity.
- Lie or post fake information.
- Share depressing and sad posts.
- Don't post only, and primarily, selfies or photos of yourself.
- Use sarcasm and humor unless you know your audience will understand/appreciate it.
- Don't post someone else's content **without asking permission first.**

When using social media, do:

- Post on a regular, consistent schedule.
- Keep your online info up to date and accurate.
- Be selective in who you approve in your social media networks.

- **Model good behavior.**
- Post positive thoughts.
- Double check spelling and grammar.
- Post what you know for a fact.
- Be supportive of others; recognize good deeds.
- Post a majority of other people in your photos.
- When posting photos, post in a link first if you want to maintain your photo copyright.
- Saying to the world someone else is honestly wonderful **has more credibility** and builds more trust than you telling the world that YOU are wonderful.

FACEBOOK

As my mother used to say, my house, my rules. Facebook is a privately-owned company, not governed by the U.S. Constitution's Freedom of Speech Amendment nor by the U.S. Government. That's been a hard pill for some people to take when they violate Facebook's rules. If you are going to be on Facebook, you will do it **by their rules or they can block and/or remove you.**

NONPROFIT FACEBOOK PAGES

If you know you are headed to being an incorporated nonprofit, then **don't use Facebook** until you are formally incorporated.

- There are a **slew of requirements** including incorporation papers, a designated legal representative and more to set up a Facebook nonprofit page.
- More importantly, if you set up just a discussion page, you **can't keep that page later** when you set up a nonprofit page.
- Focus on your meetings, emails and newsletters in the interim.

BEE CLUB FACEBOOK GROUP PAGE

Still here, I see. Well, if you insist on having a Facebook presence, it can be a good venue for people to post photos and videos with questions. However, managing these pages is high maintenance so make sure the people who are on the page **are engaging** or you may not want to invest the time that it is going to take.

There are two types of Facebook group pages: public and private. Although public pages are popular, some people prefer posting only on private pages so canvas your group to find out **which method of information sharing** they prefer.

- Once you set up the page, you **can't change** it later.
- It is helpful to have a written **Facebook managing policy**.
- Facebook itself has policies people who manage the pages have to follow. Make sure page administrators know Facebook's policies as well as those of your club.

GUIDELINES FOR RUNNING A FACEBOOK GROUP PAGE

1. Average volunteer commitment: **2-4 hours per week** depending on page activity.

2. Administrator should have experience in managing **online conflict, copyright and disparaging comments.**

3. All administrators and moderators should **sign an agreement** they will follow Facebook community policies as well as the following:

    a. The administrator will post items that **support the club's mission and programs** including links to club's website.

    b. The administrator will **not rename or otherwise alter/remove the page** without being directed to do so.

    c. The administrator will **follow best practices** for managing the page.

    d. The administrators and moderators will **not promote personal business or views.**

    e. The administrators will keep club officers informed of **any major issues** that develop.

f. The administrators will answer member private messages **within 48 hours** of being directly contacted.

DUTIES OF THE FACEBOOK GROUP PAGE ADMINISTRATOR

On Facebook itself, the administrator has the **most responsibilities.**

- The administrator is the **only person** who can delete the page.
- They are also the ones who **assign roles** to the rest of the people managing the page.
- This person is also responsible for ensuring that **no violations** of personal rights, copyrights or trademark rights occur.
- In addition, they are responsible for keeping discussions from getting out of hand, which is called derailing.

Before a Facebook administrator appoints additional persons to an administrator capacity, they should be **convinced of their trustworthiness**. People can play havoc in these positions, from stealing pages by renaming them without permission to harassing volunteers by changing their positions. Then there is the whole Facebook cop role that requires deciding when posts violate page rules. **It's not an easy job.** It takes time and good judgement, and working with other people.

- **Check with Facebook** on the latest positions and requirements because they frequently change.
- Facebook sends notices to page administrators when they make the changes.

There are a few other Facebook page jobs that may be of interest, such as page editor and moderator.

FACEBOOK PAGE EDITOR

Editors have the **same rights as administrators** but cannot distribute or revoke administrators themselves.

- They **are allowed** to edit the site, add apps, create and delete posts and comments, send messages, create advertisements and retrieve statistics.

- This role is suitable for all those **who publish daily posts and articles.**

FACEBOOK PAGE MODERATORS

Moderators are responsible for **community management.**

- Moderators **reply to and remove** comments, send messages, create advertisements and view statistics on the fan page.
- They get in touch with the people posting and moderate the discussions taking place there. If necessary, the**y can delete** inappropriate comments.
- **They cannot** post in the name of the page, and they are not able to assign roles themselves.

FACEBOOK PAGE SUGGESTED RULES

When setting up a group page, you can set rules for what is acceptable and not acceptable on your page. The following are typical Facebook page rules:

1. **Be Kind and Courteous.** We're all in this together to create a welcoming environment, learn from each other and have fun. Let's treat everyone with respect. Healthy debates are natural, but kindness is required.

2. **Respect Everyone's Privacy.** Being part of this group requires mutual trust. Authentic, expressive discussions make groups great, but may also be sensitive and private. What's shared in the group should stay in the group.

3. **No Hate Speech or Bullying.** Make sure everyone feels safe. Bullying of any kind isn't allowed, and degrading comments about things like race, religion, culture, sexual orientation, gender or identity will not be tolerated and will be deleted.

4. **No Promotions or Spam.** Give more than you take to this group. Self-promotion, spam and irrelevant links aren't allowed and will be deleted.

5. **Check Before Posting.** Posts about and supporting beekeeping are welcome. Any other posts including those asking for money, selling non-beekeeping related items, stories disproved through **fact-checking sites** and topics not related to beekeeping will be removed.

SUGGESTED FACEBOOK PAGE ADMINISTRATION POLICIES

If you choose to use Facebook for information-sharing, make it clear everyone will **need to have a Facebook account** so they can access the page. When you have some on Facebook and others not, it becomes difficult to have an effective discussion about an issue because not everyone has seen the same information shared online.

Have two people with designated access to social media and website and bank accounts at a minimum, and not from the same family. This protects the accounts, and if something happens at least one person can access the accounts and keep the club moving forward.

- If you **don't have agreement** to be on Facebook **then don't use it.**
- If you do, remember to **first email information** such as policy changes before you post on Facebook. Emailing is a more reliable tool to inform people.
- **Not everyone regularly** checks Facebook and can easily miss important, timely information.

Answer: It was Belgian writer Maurice Maeterlinck (1862-1949) in "The Life of the Bee" published in 1901 who said *"If the bee disappeared off the face of the earth, man would only have four years left to live."* He helped to spread the idea that the bee was vital to the world's ecology.

SHARING UPCOMING BEE CLUB MEETING DATES

Now that you have meeting dates and locations and have contacted your email list with the information, it is time to share information to catch other potential beekeepers. Most communities have a **variety of community calendars** from actual bulletin boards outside businesses to online forums. Here is a starting list of potential community calendar sites:

- Bookoo (there is one for most communities)
- Craigs List
- Chambers of Commerce Upcoming Meetings Calendar
- Bulletin board where you are meeting

- Beekeeping equipment business bulletin boards
- Farm and Home Center bulletin boards
- Gas station bulletin boards
- Library
- What others do you have in your community?

LOCAL RADIO, TV AND PODCASTS

If you have local newspapers, radio and TV stations or beekeepers with podcasts and websites, provide them with your meeting information. Many have **free community calendars.**

- **Provide them** with a reliable name, email and phone number in case they have questions.
- **Be prepared** in case they invite someone from your bee club for an interview.

ANNUAL BEE CLUB BENEFIT AUCTIONS

Bee clubs and associations like to use benefit auctions to raise funds. **Check with a certified public accountant** to ensure your activity is applicable for a charitable activity so the group is not responsible for sales tax. As the donator is getting something for their donation, typically only the fair market value of the donated items as determined by the donor is tax deductible NOT the amount the item brings in in a cash donation.

- To manage an auction successfully, make it clear **how the collected funds will be used.**
- Encourage **donations in advance** and
- Have **someone responsible** for collecting, and providing the items at the event where the benefit auction will be held.
- **Keep a list** of donations and donors for thank-yous.

One of the popular items to sell at benefit auctions is the **winning honey** from a honey contest.

SAMPLE BEE CLUB MEETING RADIO ANNOUNCEMENTS

This is how meeting notices can also be used for radio announcements:

1. The Eldon Bee Club will meet Saturday, January 1, 2019 at the Community Center from 2 – 4 p.m. Everyone is welcome. For more details, email ***bees@gmail.com and call (000) 000-0000.

Or

2. The Eldon Bee Club will meet Saturday, January 1, 2019 at the Community Center from 2-4 p.m. The agenda includes how to winter feed bees. Volunteers are welcome to discuss fundraising ideas. No dues. (Or donations appreciated) Refreshments will be available. For further information, visit eldonbeeclub.com, email ***bees@gmail.com and call (000) 000-0000.

SAMPLE BEE CLUB NEWS RELEASE

From Sample Bee Club

Address

Phone Number

Email and website

REGISTRATION OPEN FOR JANUARY 27, 2022 BASIC BEEKEEPING CLASS

Hometown, State, — Registration is now open for a basic beekeeping class (Day/Date/Location/Address/Time)

Cost $$ per person including lunch and class materials. Class size is limited; attendees must be at least 15 years of age or older. To register, send your name, email and phone number to SAMPLE EMAIL and a check to TREASURER **no later than (SPECIFY DATE)**

The basic beekeeping classes will include sample sample sample.

Instructors are active beekeepers

For more information about Sample Bee Club, visit samplebeeclub.com.

-end—

SAMPLE NEWSLETTER GUIDELINES

What is the newsletter objective? Newsletters should revolve around your club objectives and what **you want members to know.** Include newsletter content that is **relevant, helpful and interesting:**

- **Latest news,** ie. Passage of bees classified as livestock and no longer taxed.
- **Industry developments**, ie. Frank's bees move to Smalltown. Nancy's Ice Cream expands distribution route.
- **Frequently-asked questions.**
- "How to" articles.
- **Upcoming conference** highlights:
    - Short stories on upcoming **conference keynote speakers.**
    - **Info on contests:** honey, cooking, etc.
    - Short description of location and community where conference will be held.
    - **Recognize** volunteers helping with the event.
- **Feature stories about members.** If you have awards, have **feature stories about award nominees**, then follow-up with stories about winners.
- **Upcoming** classes/events/feature stories.
- In general,
    - **Keep feature stories** between 400-500 words. Other articles should be 200-300 words.
    - **Ask for** both horizontal and vertical photos per feature story; two of each so editor has some choices. Sizing no less than 300 dpi and originals, not photoshopped.
    - Include one or two **calls to action:** volunteer to help, join the club.
    - Consider **photo feature page** featuring an event or activity.
    - Add **letters to the editor** section to get leads on story ideas.

SAMPLE MINOR PHOTO RELEASE FORM

I, _____, the parent or legal guardian of _____ [Child] grant _____ [Party Receiving Permission] my permission to use the photographs described as (describe photographs) _____ _____ for any legal use, including but not limited to: publicity, copyright purposes, illustration, advertising, and web content.

I understand that no royalty, fee or other compensation shall become payable to me by reason of such use.

Parent/Guardian's Signature: _____ Date _____

Parent/Guardian's Printed Name: _____

Child's Printed Name: _____

Parent's Phone Number: _____

Received by (Club Representative) _____

Date_____

_____

Keep in club record official files for future reference.

Photo taking tip: If you haven't asked permission first, frame your photos so you can't identify the subjects. It's relatively easy to do with beekeepers in bee suits!

A NOTE ABOUT GIVING MEDICAL ADVICE

It's uncomfortable to be sitting at a club meeting listening to a non-medical person tell someone their child will outgrow an allergic reaction. Besides being inappropriate, you are putting other people in harm's way. My best suggestion about giving medical advice is: **DON'T**.

- If you are interested in the history to some of the medical practices as well as studies, go to original sources. Get the correct information.

- And then still DON'T give medical advice. Unless you are a knowledgeable health specialist. Even then, that does not guarantee the health professional has the background to address your questions. Ask **what experience they have** before you do what they suggest.

- And as far as you giving medical advice, see above.

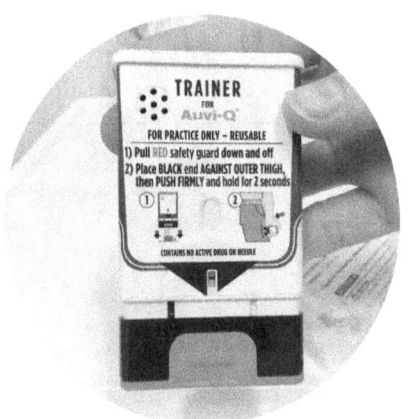

*Most pharmacies have **injection trainers** to demonstrate the correct way to use an EpiPen®.*

DID YOU KNOW?

- In their 6-8 week lifespan, a worker honey bee will fly the equivalent distance of 1½ times the circumference of the Earth.

- For every pound of honey produced, a hive must collect 10 pounds of pollen.

- Honey made from rhododendron is poisonous through rarely fatal.

(Courtesy of Beepods.com)

CHAPTER 12

Meeting Online

"I can compare clarity to pruning in gardening. You know, you need to be clear. If you are not clear, nothing is going to happen. You have to be clear. Then you have to be confident about your vision. And after that, you just have to put a lot of work in."

— *Diane von Furstenberg, U.S. fashion designer and entrepreneur*

The COVID 19 coronavirus worldwide pandemic has **significantly altered** the way groups get together. As the COVID variants spread through the US through close personal contact, it is still unclear what the future holds. The good news is that the basics of organizing a club are still the same. Clubs need mailing lists, programs to inform and educate, and beekeepers willing to help others.

The big difference today is how we connect. The following are several options for holding online meetings. **Try one as a test** and determine which one best fits your club's finances and club members:

*Use that collection of beekeeping books to **elevate your computer** so that you are sitting at eye level for online meetings. Just kidding, your cookbook collection will work just as well!*

SOME EXAMPLES OF ONLINE MEETING PLATFORMS (AS OF 2022)

- **FreeConferenceCall.com.** Donation based, focused on serving students and nonprofits, they include suggested donation amounts.
- **GotoMeeting.com** $12/month for 150 participants.
- **Skype.com.** Free meetings up to 50 participants; recordings that last 30 days.
- **Zoom.com** Free for 40-minute meetings; $150/yr for up to 100 participants. There may be discount coupons available for a yearlong subscription.
- **Google Meet.**

When **using these online services**:

- Make sure all other windows are **closed.**
- If the signal becomes wonky, **take it off video** and only use the audio to minimize bandwidth use.
- Inclement weather can also **impact the quality** of the connection.

ONLINE MEETING SET UP

Running an online meeting requires a **different approach** and **more pre-meeting planning.**

- **Set up your computer camera** so that it is straight on or a little higher than where you are sitting. You want to be talking to people, not down, or up, to them.
- Use **natural lighting** when possible. When meeting evenings, use lights around your face, not to the side or behind you.
- Check your **visual and audio background** to make sure it is not too busy or distracting.
- **Turn off** any machine, like dehumidifiers and such, during your meeting; your microphone will amplify the sound they make.

- **Test and get familiar** with computer microphones. When all else fails, participants will hear you so make sure the sound quality is the best it can be. Adding a microphone may improve the sound quality.
- Consider using **ear buds** to better hear everyone participating.

DRESS REHEARSE ONLINE MEETING

If you haven't used any of these platforms, have **a dress rehearsal** with meeting helpers so you all get familiar with how to get things done.

ONLINE MEETING MANAGERS

Assign roles so everyone knows what they are supposed to do during the meeting, usually 4 people:
- Help with meeting log-in
- Tech support **during the meeting**
- Chat room **monitoring**
- Who will be making presentations and on what topics
- Have a **backup way to communicate** during the meeting such as texting.

PREPARING FOR ONLINE MEETINGS

I know some clubs are used to winging club meetings but online sessions require a little **more pre-meeting organization** to be successful.
- Prepare, coordinate and **share an agenda** prior to the meeting with background information so everyone knows what to expect and what roles they play.
- Keep online business meetings to a maximum of one hour if at all possible.
- Take a 10-minute break if going longer.
- Allow for an **informal conversational time** for participants to share and ask questions.

ONLINE MEETING MANAGEMENT

The meeting host should **turn off** all computer notifications and close all programs on their computer. This will improve bandwidth and ensure the smoothest transmission of audio and video.

- To open the call, ask everyone to **use the chat box** to say hello. It is a good way to get people focused and comfortable with technology.
- Request that all board members **use and turn on their video camera** (if they have one), so everyone can be seen and heard during the meeting.
- Let participants know that the **board chair will recognize them** before speaking to avoid everyone talking at once.
- Ask everyone to **use their mute button** when they're not speaking to silence background noises from kids, pets and others working at home.
- Set **agreed-upon maximum speaking times** for each topic and speaker to ensure you can efficiently and effectively get through your agenda.
- Assign a **meeting management person** to serve as timekeeper.

Consider using the chat box, poll and quiz functions to enhance the efficiency of your meeting:

- **Use the chat box** to ask for a motion, second and other brief responses.
- **Use a poll** for yes/no questions and asking for feedback on proposed actions, such as "What suggestions do you have to improve future online meetings?"
- For a mission moment, **create a quiz** using three fast facts about your organization's impact, such as the number of people served last year or the cost to help one family.
- During the last five minutes, **ask everyone for a closing thought,** or ask what worked well and what still needs improvement.

Note: Some groups keep both the chat box and the Q&A boxes open during a presentation. I close the chat box and keep the Q&A box open so the speaker, and/or facilitator, can quickly see, monitor and answer questions.

Plus everyone should be listening to the presentation!

ONLINE MEETING DO'S AND DON'TS

For an efficient online meeting, **do:**

- Provide detailed financial statements, committee reports, meeting minutes and other information **prior to the meeting.** A week in advance is a good rule of thumb.
- Use **simple slides** to advance your meeting agenda and highlight key data points being discussed.
- Use **transition slides** to keep attendees on track, such as a consent agenda, action items, financial discussion, etc. to frame your meeting.
- Allow **extra time for questions** throughout the meeting. People may need more time to process the information being shared, and it will take longer to hear and respond to questions.
- **Use white backgrounds** and easy-to-read black or dark fonts of 14-point or higher.
- Add a **phone number or email** to the bottom of each slide for participants to contact regarding technical problems without interrupting the meeting.
- Provide a **written record** of the meeting in addition to post-meeting access to a meeting recording for those who missed the meeting.
- **Thank** those who are helping both in front of cameras and behind.

Now some things to not do if you want a good meeting:

- Don't **fill slides with text;** just show the key points on your slides.
- **Don't use animation in slides.** They can interfere with the audio based on each user's Internet speed.
- Don't **spring new topics.** If you have to, present the topic early in the meeting and specify when it will be brought back up for discussion and a vote.
- Give participants time to think about the topic and the information you shared.
- What else **has not worked well** for you in an online meeting?

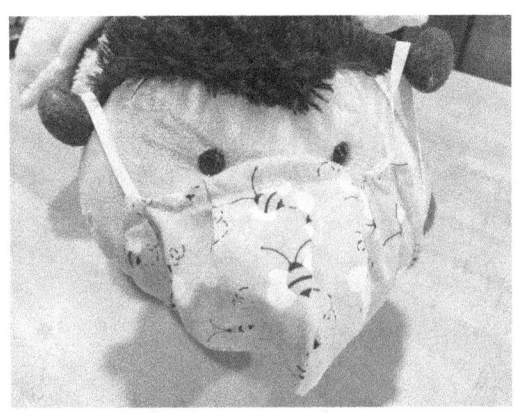

*When meeting in person with another beekeeper, remember to **wear a mask** to protect both of you and not pass on the COVID virus.*

HOW TO KEEP CLUB GOING WHEN NOT MEETING

There are parts of the US where internet service is so poor, or non-existent, that online meetings are not an option. Regardless of the reason why you can't go online to meet:

- **Develop a calling tree.** Each person takes two names and calls and/or texts those names to check up on them, find out how their bees are doing, offer support.
- **Send plain emails.** Keep them simple so they won't take an inordinate time to download. No photos or graphics, just plain text writing.
- **Increase email frequency.** Provide information about upcoming beekeeping tasks, area events of interest, information about club members.
- **Use the Buddy system.** Encourage everyone to have a "bee buddy" who can support each other.

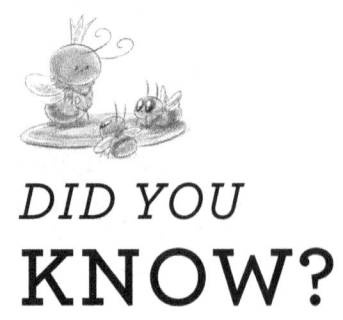

DID YOU KNOW?

- On average, Americans consume 1.31 pounds of honey every year.
- There are estimated to be nearly 212,000 beekeepers in the United States.
- Honey is the only foodstuff that contains all of the necessary nutrients to sustain life.

(Courtesy of Beepods.com)

CHAPTER 13

Changing Laws

"In the end, laws are agreements that communities forge among their members, and beekeepers are valuable members of these precious communities. We can influence these laws without being lawyers or politicians, but by being participants in the community and guardians of beekeeping's role in the latter."

— Toni Burham, Washington D.C. Beekeeper, Bee Culture Magazine June 27, 2016
"The Quest for the Model Urban Bee Law"

As more people become aware of the role of pollinators, legislators are **facing citizen proposals** to change the way they classify, and manage, lawns and public spaces as well as where beekeeping is an acceptable practice.

One of the targets of change is a group of plants called "weeds." **Weeds** are defined as "plants that are not valued where they are growing" and "usually have a vigorous growth." Combined with a post WWII nationwide movement to have green carpet-like lawns, communities adopted a range of laws that encouraged manicured green spaces at the cost of plant diversity. Some also prohibited where property owners could grow what plants, such as vegetable beds on front lawns.

Research confirms those expanses of green are barren of any contributions back to the ecosystem and are expensive and high maintenance. There are an estimated 40 to 50 million acres of lawn in the US: 40% is residential lawns, 20% lines roadsides, and about 3% is on golf courses.

As more land gets developed, there will be a **decrease in available food pollinators depend on**, contributing to their decline and extinction. It may **also affect us**. One out of every three bites of healthy food we eat is courtesy of pollinators.

The same kind of challenge is facing communities trying to **manage where bees are kept.** Running the gamut from outright prohibiting beekeeping to specifying how many hives can be kept per acre, these laws tend to be complaint-driven as opposed to in the best interests of all parties. Much like beekeeping itself, appropriate laws "depend" on a combination of factors and considerations.

HOW TO MAKE CHANGES IN LAWS

Making legislative changes can be challenging. Besides going against accepted practices, new laws can inadvertently impact others. I know what it's like to be **on both sides** of those proposals. For many years I made a number of suggestions to our local government for nonprofits I started, beginning with an animal shelter in 1979. Then for 8 years I sat on that same government entity listening to others make their proposed changes and improvements. I also worked in Washington D.C. for many years tracking legislation and providing information. In 2015, I worked with a Missouri State Beekeepers Association team to change Missouri's honey labeling laws.

The good news is the process is the same; the challenge is finding out what laws you need to change, who to know, and **who supports** the concept you are proposing.

UNDERSTAND LAWS "ON THE BOOKS"

There are a number of laws at various government levels. First, understand who is imposing what limitations, or requirements:

- At the local government level, laws are usually enacted because someone complained. **Complaint-driven laws** can be the messiest ones if the local governmental entity hasn't carefully researched the proposed law implications. Usually those get enacted because no one else is challenging the reason, and the possible implications, of those laws. Small local governments usually don't have the time, or staff, to do the research before they respond to someone's complaint.

- **State laws** are regulations imposed on smaller governmental entities. Some may or may not impact and affect your community depending on the size of your community.

- **Federal laws** are regulations that often impact states across the country.

MAKING THE CHANGE

The following are some of my suggestions on **how to prepare yourself**, and take on, making changes. These principles will work for the various levels of government with the focus on your local government.

1. **Do your homework.** You are going to be the "voice' of the proposed change you want made. You need to know as much as, if not more than anyone else, about every aspect of the proposal. You will need to:

    a. **Research and know** your local ordinances. Check with your city clerk to get a good starting point.

    b. **Understand** how your local governing body operates.

    c. **Know your state laws** and how they impact your community.

    d. Identify the **alternative(s) you want.**

    e. Make sure your alternative(s) **will "fit" your community.**

    f. **Take photos** to "show" the change you want made. Better yet, have a demonstration of what you are proposing. Some people are not exposed to alternatives so make it easy for them to understand what you are proposing. Something visual is much easier to understand than a long description.

    g. Remember to do an **inventory of your own practices.** If you yourself are not following what you propose, it won't take much to defeat it.

    h. If you have the means, **talk to a lawyer** about the proposed language you want to use. Smaller governmental entities may not have a full-time lawyer or only use one on retainer. Getting your proposal language in final form may give you a leg up when you make your proposal.

2. **Identify who will challenge proposed changes.** Knowing who may oppose you may help you assess how difficult, or easy, it will be to make the changes you are proposing. **Who may be opposed and why?**

a. Start with **the most impacted.** How do the neighbors feel about the proposed changes, are they supportive of your efforts? One of the easiest steps you can take is to set up a demonstration somewhere – your own property or a local nearby school or vacant property. **Put up signs** explaining what you are doing. A number of national groups offer attractive signs that can be part of your effort to educate people.

b. Are opponents the people who will vote on your requested changes? **Spend time with them** to understand their opposition. Educate them on why your proposal is something they should support.

c. You will also find a percentage of people who don't understand. **Education** is the best approach before you make a proposal; enlisting the support of well-respected community members can help increase understanding and backing.

d. Another group may be opposed because the change impacts them directly. If you can substantiate how your proposal **will benefit them** – less work, less cost, possible voter support – you will get the attention of this group.

e. A percentage of opposition will be from people who **don't like change. Set those names aside** because you may have enough support to get your proposal approved without them. In general, people who don't like change are a tough group to convince otherwise.

f. If you are engaging with opponents, identify who they are and **prepare how you will address their concerns.** Is there someone else who can talk to them besides you? Do you have arguments to address their concerns? As with a lot of things in life, it is who you know that can make a difference.

g. Are opponents the people who will vote on your requested changes? **Spend time with them** to understand their opposition. Educate them on why your proposal is something they should support.

3. **Know how your government works.**

   a. Spend extra time **getting to know** how your government works and how proposals get reviewed and approved.

b. **Discuss with city government officials** one on one. Identify their concerns and **note how you will address them.**

c. Make sure to include and address their concerns in your **one-page summary.**

d. Check if your community has **mandatory and/or volunteer-related programs** such as Missouri's Bee Check, a voluntary hive registration program. It may not be directly related to your issue but you may be asked about it. Knowing about these kinds of programs helps to establish your credibility.

e. **Check with other groups** that have approached your government to make changes; learn from their experience and follow their advice.

4. **Identify who may support changes.** Just as important as knowing your opponents, you need to identify those individuals and groups **who will support you.** You may need to call on them to help you with your proposal. Are they

   a. Neighbors?

   b. City officials?

   c. Community groups?

   If they look like the same groups that could be opposed, **they could be.** It is up to you to know who the principal influencers and decision-makers are and where key individuals stand. The more you know about the critical players in these groups, the more successful you will be getting your proposal approved.

5. **Prepare yourself.** You need to know your proposal so well that you are **talking about it in your sleep.** Here are some things you can do **to prepare yourself:**

   a. Develop a **one-page summary** of issue/proposed solution. Include photos!

   b. Practice an elevator speech, which is a **15-second, easy to understand pitch.** What are you proposing and why?

   c. **Practice a media interview.** Who/what/where/when/why/with whom/how much. Keep your answers short. Summarize.

6. Depending on other factors, such as when your supporters can help, **set up a contact calendar.**

    a. Making changes **can take time.**

    b. Having a calendar of who you will contact when will keep you focused and help you make the meetings and other related events that will require your time.

7. Once you feel you are ready, develop a second list of **potential key contacts.** The first names on your key contact list should be **your supporters.**

    a. **Neighbors ok?** Make sure to have their support. Pass out one page summary copies to them. Get them organized and ready to help you with emails, attending meetings, making phone calls, answering questions.

    b. **Talk to other support groups. Identified other groups that agree with you?** Ask them to attend/email and show support. Some groups pass resolutions showing their collective support of proposals. Depending on your timeline, get on their schedule to debate and vote on your proposal.

    c. One of the more popular approaches to show support is to **circulate petitions.** Don't focus on numbers; make sure the signatures are from people who understand the issue and **truly support it.** It's not how many people sign a petition but who signs.

8. **Make your case/presentation.** Ready to make your proposal? Know what the **meeting rules are and follow them:**

    a. Pass out one page summary of issue/proposed solution (with photos)

    b. Listen to discussion; take notes on who is supporting you.

    c. Encourage support groups to attend meetings with you.

    d. Observe time limits.

    e. Dress professionally.

    f. Follow-up one on one with supporters.

    g. Track your issue.

9. **Be ready to work with media.**

    Sometimes there is a tendency to go straight to media with an issue. I recommend you talk to **potential supporters and voters first**. Sometimes getting media support can appear as pressuring a governmental entity and that can strain the working relationship.

    On the other hand, most government meetings have local media attending. If you don't know who they are before you attend the meeting, **introduce yourself** during a meeting break and get their names and contact information. Be ready to provide yours.

    a. Give media your **one-page summary** of issue/proposed solution (with photos)

    b. Be prepared to **answer questions.**

    c. **If you don't know, say so,** then follow up with the information they requested.

10. **Track your proposal.**

    One presentation will not usually do it so you need to **shepherd your presentation.** Keep your calendar updated and follow up on any requests for information.

    a. Follow-up with elected supporters. Ask them for their help and thank them along the way. Keep asking what happens next.

    b. **Count your votes**. Know how many votes you need and where you are in getting those votes.

    c. Be patient with the process but **keep after it.**

    d. Provide updates; keep answering questions and keep in contact with your supporters.

    e. Track other communities discussing **similar issues and proposed legislative changes.** Their experiences may give you ideas and suggestions for your community.

    f. **Don't get stuck** on only one answer. Raising the questions and issues may generate even better solutions. Listen. Be open to suggestions.

With **time and persistence,** you should be able to make the improvements you want made.

Your Notes

_____

_____

_____

_____

_____

_____

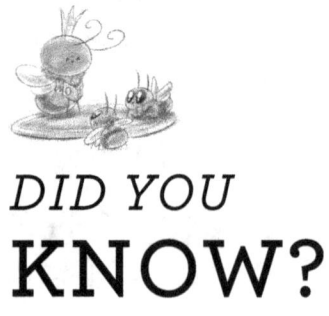

DID YOU KNOW?

- The perfect hexagons that form honeycomb hold the most amount of honey with the smallest amount of material (wax).

- There are people in Africa that keep elephants out of their fields by keeping honey bee hives around the fields in what is called a "bee fence."

- While bears do enjoy honey, they prefer to eat bee larvae for the protein.

(Courtesy of Beepods.com)

CHAPTER 14

Working Partnerships

"It takes two flints to make a fire."

— *Louisa May Alcott, (1832-1888) American novelist*

Let's face it, getting much done as an individual, or an organization, is much better working as a team. One of the ways nonprofit educational bee clubs can get more accomplished is by **working with partners.** Working partnerships bring two or more groups together to achieve a common purpose or goal.

- Look for other organizations that share **similar goals** and interests.
- **Strike up a conversation** with your leadership about approaching them; then
- **Find someone in their leadership** who can be approached about potentially working together.

DEFINE WHAT YOU EACH BRING TO THE TABLE

To be a successful working partner, it is **important to define** what each of the parties is contributing. Working partnerships are not necessarily an equal division of power, expenses and responsibilities.

With detailed discussions and good communication, it's more **what each partner is/can offer** to meet the mutual goals.

WORKING PARTNERSHIP BETWEEN LANDOWNER AND BEEKEEPER

When I was secretary of a state association, one of the most-asked questions was how to get landowners and beekeepers to work together for their mutual benefit.

Farmers often use beekeeping pollination services to increase their crop yields. Those "contracts" are easy because the farmer pays the beekeeper to provide a service.

But what if you have some land you want to offer a nearby beekeeper as potential bee foraging area. In the years I tried to facilitate these discussions, I found that

- Some **landowners don't know** the financial investment beekeepers make to keep bees. They expected beekeepers to do all of the work for free while the landowners netted all of the honey profit.
- Beekeepers appreciated the offer of possibly new bee foraging areas. They didn't feel the landowners **were taking a similar financial investment, and risk**, as the beekeepers.
- In two cases, the landowners wanted to charge the beekeepers to place hives on their properties.

In any working partnership, think about **fairness** and **sharing the load.** Working partnerships should be beneficial for both landowners and beekeepers.

GOOD WORKING PARTNERSHIP EXAMPLE

To start off this working partnership, one way to be fair and to share the load would be to split the cost for the beekeeping equipment and cost of the bees. That way both sides are going into the working partnership on an equal footing. Then

- **Beekeepers contribute managing** the bee colonies through the season.
- **Landowners offer access** to their land.
- At the end of the season, the two agree to **spli**t any honey.

I have a beekeeping friend who keeps hives on someone else's property. At the end of the season, he shares the honey bounty. It's not something they discussed but they were lucky, both sides are happy with this sweet arrangement.

INFORMAL AGREEMENTS

In general, informal working agreements work well if both parties know, respect and trust each other. Even then it's a good idea to **have a written record** of what each side expects out of the association.

- If the parties don't know each other, or are just getting to know each other, **write details down.**
- **Document** what each party will do and what happens to the beekeeping equipment, and bees, should either party bow out of the arrangement.
- The process of writing things down will give each party the opportunity to develop an understanding of the arrangements.

MEMORANDUMS OF UNDERSTANDING

One way organizations **formalize working partnerships** is with **memorandums of understanding. (MOU)** These documents

- Outline what each working partner will do and contribute.
- They are not legally binding.
- They often are the first step to developing a contract.

Some organizations use MOUs to establish a framework for how working partner agencies will work towards a common goal. They are often helpful to have when partners are working together when applying for grant funding.

The following page is a sample MOU.

When planning events with partners, include how you plan to help get participants around the event. **Renting golf carts** *provide an easy form of transportation.*

SAMPLE MEMORANDUM OF UNDERSTANDING

This Memorandum of Understanding (MOU) is entered into, by and between (list working partners) partners of the Missourians for Monarchs (Collaborative), working under the laws and authorities of (state) whose mission is (list mission.)

RESPONSIBILITIES OF WORKING PARTNERS

The working partners mutually agree to:

1. To support the goal(s) of_____
2. To work together by: (joint meetings, sharing assets, supporting an event(s)
3. To annually the progress towards the mutually-agreed upon goal(s).
4. If there are financial contributions, those are usually covered in a separate document.
5. This working partnership will continue until _____ and/or be renewed (ie. annually)
6. Signatures and dates of each party representative.
7. List of working parties and their representatives.

_____

End of Sample MOU

FORMAL CONTRACTS

Formal contracts detail what each party will do including:
- Who provides equipment
- Who maintains the apiary
- What chemicals are allowed

- What happens if bees die

You will find excellent contract examples online from University Extension offices. As usual, check with an attorney before signing.

WORKING PARTNERS CHARTER

Just as you set up a charter for your beginning bee club, you also set up a **working partnership** charter.
- **Keep it simple** and clear.
- Spell out measurable **expectations** and
- **Who is responsible** for being each partner's point of contact.

LIAISON WORKING PARTNERSHIP POSITIONS

Liaison positions are working partnership positions that are excellent for larger bee clubs dealing with hundreds of members. These positions can focus on specific groups and club activities that support and help the club reach their goals.

- **Military liaison positions,** for example, help address issues active and retired military, and their dependents, may have. These persons should have military background so they can help the military with their unique issues.
- **Partnership liaisons** focus on key relationships and help to develop new ones. Because this is a position much too easy to expand, it's a good idea to have a job description defining the role of the position, and the partners.
- **Transportation liaisons** concentrate on providing ways for members and/or attendees to move around meetings and/or events.

    a. This position is **handy to have** if you are picking up bees, distributing bees, working a conference spread across a campus and/or in several buildings.

    b. It **will cost less** to make arrangements for transportation support prior to the event than during the event.

    c. Identify what needs you may have early and make those arrangements. Include signage and clear directions to participants prior to the event.

I have had partnership liaison positions at several organizations. The position can very easily become a catchall for other administrative work. It's helpful to have a job description that outlines duties and responsibilities, reporting deadlines and the term of the appointment. It helps to also define goals so that accomplishments can be measured.

SAMPLE PARTNERSHIP LIAISON

Approved on this date by the Executive Board: _____

The Partnership Liaison serves an important function by serving as the communication conduit with strategic partners. Current strategic partnerships have been previously identified or secured through ongoing memberships with national or regional apicultural groups, or through the execution of Memorandums of Understanding (MOUs) with other entities or organizations directly or indirectly.

Duties and Responsibilities. Partnership Liaison will routinely facilitate communication between current strategic partners. This may involve telephone or conference calls, email messages or letters, and occasional attendance at vital meetings. The Partnership Liaison shall confine their role to such current strategic partners and future partners as directed by the executive committee.

Strategic Partners. (Current strategic partners are listed.)

Additionally, the Partnership Liaison serves to maintain such strategic partnership relationships through ongoing dialogue and updates, seeking clarifications to questions, and otherwise keeping one another apprised of concurrent obligations, and current matters affecting one another.

Other individuals may be designated from time to time to assist in fulfilling this vital responsibility. Regular updates and reports should be submitted in writing, or whenever requested to do so, but at least bi-annually.

The volunteer appointment is for 1 year; renewable year to year.

(end of Sample Partnership Liaison Position)

OPPORTUNITIES FOR WORKING PARTNERSHIPS

Working partnerships are excellent opportunities for a **variety of reasons.** By doubling up and working towards the same goals, small groups can often get more done.

Partnerships offer **opportunity to pool funds** and get more accomplished, such as
- Annual Conferences
- Annual Field Days
- Annual Bee "Fun" Days
- Work days

Working partnerships also work well for working together on
- Beekeeping classes
- Ordering supplies including bees and queen bees
- Queen Bee Rearing

EVENT, MARKETING, VOLUNTEER, AND VENDOR COORDINATORS

There are other club roles that may **require someone dedicated to those particular functions**, similar to partnership liaisons, especially if you are a larger club. The following are some examples of the positions that can be set up similar to partnership liaison positions with specific job descriptions:

- **Event Coordinators** are responsible for coordinating all of the details associated with a special event.
- **Marketing Coordinators use magic to share information.** Oh, you're still with me? Okay so it's not magic but many people don't understand this function, or the amount of time and effort it takes to do it well. It can be measured but not necessarily for free. Set clear expectations.
- **Volunteer Coordinators** match volunteers with club jobs that need to get done.
- **Vendor Coordinators** work with businesses interested in having a booth or some form presence at an event so they can offer information and/or products for sale.

LIABILITY "WAIVERS"

In general, liability waivers are often misunderstood. Liability waivers do not protect against lawsuits. They are more a means to inform someone about potential risks.

- **Signing a waiver doesn't protect you** from being sued or
- **Prevent someone** from suing you.

What it does do is make the person signing the waiver **aware of what potential risks** they may be. They sign the waiver to indicate they have read and understood the potential risks.

Liability provisions vary from state to state so check first with your friendly attorney.

KEEP KIDS IN MIND

Every once in awhile a parent or guardian may bring a child to a meeting. **Keep a box of crayons and coloring sheets** in your files so you can provide some entertainment.

It's also an opportunity to share bee facts with a future potential beekeeper!

DID YOU **KNOW?**

- ⬡ Honey bees don't sleep. Instead, they spend their nights motionless, conserving energy for the next day's activities.
- ⬡ For every pound of honey produced, a colony must collect 10 pounds of pollen.
- ⬡ Bees use the sun as a compass, and on cloudy days, use polarized light to find their way.

(Courtesy of Beepods.com)

CHAPTER 15

Stepping Away

"Human beings have fabricated the illusion that in the 21st century they have the technological prowess to be independent of nature. Bees underline the reality that we are more, not less, dependent on nature's services in a world of close to 7 billion people."

— Achim Steiner, (1961-present) Executive Director UN Environment Programme

Retirement is a scary word. I have friends who declare they are "never going to retire," asserting this after complaining to me for years that they love what they have been doing and they can't imagine doing anything else. I sometimes question their creativity. As someone who has started yet another chapter in my life, I can attest the R word is anything but scary. With advanced planning and goals met, this chapter is about **having new adventures** and **learning new things.** One of my beekeeping students turned mentor likes to say there are days he wishes he was back at work just so that he can get a day off. That is so true!

One of the best pieces of advice I ever heard given to someone considering retirement was to **find a hobby first**. Knowing how focused some people can be in their work lives, that is excellent advice although I for one can't remember the last time I was bored. I suppose living with inquisitive cats may have something to do with that.

*When giving away items at a meeting drawing, **thank everyone who donates,** that may encourage future donations. Include pollinator plants and items for bees as well as beekeepers and their significant others. Winning something lovely and handmade is a nice benefit of non-beekeepers keeping someone company at a bee club meeting!*

Part of the advantage of having a bee club structure, defined duties and responsibilities as well as reliable, dependable people is that you can "retire." Another beekeeping friend calls this an **"exit strategy."**

MAKING A SMOOTH TRANSITION

If you have ever been part of an organization with what I call "leadership hiccups," you know **a little advance planning** will cure those. Most organizations build that into their structure; others just take new people on and hope for the best. The latter are the organizations that tend to veer the farthest away from their stated mission and, in most cases, get the least amount done.

As you plan your bee club, make sure:

- There is a **clear trajectory** through the club positions if someone wants to take on additional duties;
- That each has an **expiration date** (terms) and
- That there is a **defined end** to their formal involvement.

I know several past club presidents who have to take a year off after the end of their terms before they can re-engage. Club **leadership can be challenging and exhausting.**

Knowing there are limits to the time in each position makes them less scary, so more people may consider filing the positions. Having an end is also **a motivator** to get things done before time runs out.

TACKLING THE HARD STUFF

Having been on the motivating end of terms, I also found that there is one more significant contribution that can be made, and that is tackling the hard stuff.

1. **Bylaw Changes.** Although most groups may work hard at first to get the Bylaws just right, circumstances may suggest needed updates and few people I know willing will tackle that challenging job. Some of the best Bylaw revision people I have ever worked with were past presidents who brought their extensive group knowledge to the table and were able to improve the rules.

2. **Honest Talk.** Being kind does not mean not addressing issues. If there is something that needs to be discussed, think it through:

    a. Who is the best person to raise the issue besides yourself.

    b. Who can be trusted to support the person with the issue.

    c. What outcome do you want to generate by addressing it.

    d. What is the fallout if it is not addressed.

    If you are on your way out, you may be the best person to take this on. **Don't do it in a vacuum,** discuss it with the president and whoever else needs to be involved.

    Same thing applies to organizational issues. If you have been ignoring something that is getting worse and not addressing it, think it through and tackle it. You want to leave the bee club **in the best condition** you can for your successor.

    If you are not sure what to do about it, **discuss it with the rest of your club officers,** you may be surprised that they not only know all about it but have some sound recommendations.

3. **Legacy.** In my former corporate life, I observed a number of professionals making interesting decisions just to have their name left on something. **The best legacy** anyone can leave is capable, successful people carrying on their work and contributions so invest in good people and the rest will follow.

4. **Awards.** Although it is commendable when organizations create special awards for people who are leaving, there is also a downside. People who are leaving may be unforgettable and indispensable but they should not be irreplaceable. If the bee club has been well established, the **functions should continue smoothly** as volunteers leave and new people move in. The transition should be a tribute to their ongoing contributions making the bee club sustainable. By making a special award, though, an organization can be diluting the effect working together creates so establish awards that recognize mission contributions.

RECOGNITION AWARDS

Some bee clubs have annual awards; others prefer to let the community individually support and recognize people on their own. If you choose to have awards, studies show that there is a significant **generational difference** in how **people react to awards.** The shift is basically from honoring time devoted or accomplishment-based to everyone being recognized, which in my view negates the reason to have awards.

Awards can do a number of things:
- They can **motivate people;**
- **Recognize measurable contributions** and
- **Help new members** understand what is expected of them.
- The foundation of awards programs addresses the basic **human need to be accepted.**

From an organizational perspective, awards **provide milestones** that help define and communicate the behavior that contributes to more universal acceptance.

On the other hand, awards just to make someone happy can be counter-productive, especially if the award seems to support inappropriate behavior or poor character. What is it that Dr. Phil McGraw likes to say, don't reward bad behavior?

DEVELOPING AN AWARDS PROGRAM

If you are rewarding the kind of behavior you want to continue in your bee club, **keep this in mind:**
- **Clearly spell out** what someone should have accomplished to receive a particular award over a defined period of time.
- **Tie all awards** to the bee club's mission.
- **Minimize** making up "special" awards where only one individual qualifies. You want awards to be attainable by most members.
- **Keep it simple.** The more awards you give out, the more you water down the honor.
- Someone **besides the recipient** should make the nomination.

Awards should also be **open to most of members** and not focused on bee club leadership. Some clubs even specifically eliminate their leadership from awards categories to encourage nominations.

In addition to a generational shift in giving out awards, the awards themselves have taken a different turn. I can remember when retirees where given retirement watches, which have made way for retirement blankets and choose your own award programs.

Keep it simple and clear so the point of the awards are **not lost in the details.**

*It was great **fun to surprise** my bee buddy David Draker with Missouri State Beekeepers Association 2020 Mentor of the Year Award. As a treat, I gave him a bottle of wine one of our students had shared with us as a thank you for helping them. And yes, I put off sharing the wine with him until the award winners were announced!*

AWARD EXAMPLES

The following are examples of typical award categories that support bee club missions:

- **Beekeeper of the Year:** awarded to a bee club beekeeper who has done the most to support the bee club mission in the past year.
- **Young Beekeeper of the Year:** awarded to a beekeeper 21 years and younger who has contributed to advancing the bee club's mission in the past year.
- **Mentor of the Year:** awarded to a bee club beekeeper who exemplifies the values of a mentor in the past year.
- There is another popular category that does not reflect the communal aspect of a bee club, **Volunteer of the Year.** Although I appreciate the sentiment behind this award, I don't recommend it for an all-volunteer organization where so many people contribute.

If you want to have volunteer recognition of an individual who has gone above and beyond, recognize them in one of the already listed categories.

MAKE AWARDS PRACTICAL

If you are going to give out awards, make it more than a piece of paper or a plaque, make it practical:

- **An embossed hive tool** with the recipient's name and award date;
- **Honey jars or honey dippers** for honey tasting contest winners;
- **A smoker** for a beekeeper of the year and young beekeeper of the year.

By making the award visible and tangible, you are letting others see the recognition and motivating those to also **follow in the awardee footsteps.**

ANNOUNCING YOU ARE LEAVING

Once you make the decision to leave, let the club president **know first in private.** That will give the president time to think about the implications of your leaving and who can be tapped to fill in.

Unless there is a pressing reason to drop and run, give the organization time to adjust to the news and find someone to move into your position. Depending on what you do, **offer to train the next person** so that they have support.

Finally work out **when you will share with the group** that you are leaving.

- **Don't announce** a departure in the middle of your bee club's largest annual event, for example. Any leadership departure can be misconstrued, even if there is no connection between your departure and the event.
- If you have people associated with social media accounts, ask them to **give advance notice** before they drop off the accounts leaving no one having access to those accounts.
- Prioritize who you are telling and when. Your executive committee **should hear first** before the rest of your club.
- Helps also to tell your spouse and/or **family first.**

TWO KINDS OF KNOWLEDGE

The most challenging transition of someone leaving is what they take with them. There are usually **two kinds** of organizational knowledge:

- Formal knowledge and background:
- On-the-job experience.

FORMAL KNOWLEDGE AND BACKGROUND

If you are the person leaving, **pass on copies of your files and records**. If no one has been selected or stepped into your position, give the records to the bee club secretary.

If someone refuses to share records, try to **find out why.** You may uncover a deeper issue that needs to be addressed with the next person in the same position.

ON-THE-JOB EXPERIENCE

Although it is helpful to have previous records, the most challenging knowledge to capture, and loose, is the on-the-job experience.

To make a smooth transition, **plan for time between the person leaving and the new person coming on board.** It doesn't have to be long but the overlap will ensure that some of this knowledge won't get lost.

- In addition, the incoming person will tend to transition faster because they had time with their predecessor and could ask questions.
- If you are the new person coming in, **ask a lot of "why" questions** before recommending changes. Knowing why some things are done will help you be more successful in your term as you make your recommendations.
- If you are the person leaving, share the background to your recommendations. Adding context to why you suggest certain changes will help the next person.

The objective of all of this is to **capture knowledge**, not repeat previous mistakes, and to **continue to build** on what has worked well.

DON'T SHOOT THE MESSENGER

Sometimes new leadership will ask for input from existing members and then argue the input and, worse, berate members who engage. **Be very careful** of this approach or you may find yourself in a vacuum for the rest of your term and guaranteed to fail.

New leadership holds a promise of changes and improvements as well as being motivational so **handle responses carefully**:

- If you are asking the questions, be ready for both positive and negative answers.
- Address the negatives that are holding the group back;
- Build on the positives.

RESPECT WISHES

I have seen a number of situations where the organization tried to impose an event on someone who wanted to quietly fade away. Instead of an amicable separation, the person left angry and with little good to say about the organization. The same applies to public recognition so **have a policy** in place so everyone knows what to expect.

- If you do a story about one retiree from your bee club, make sure to **offer that to all others** who retire. I watched one organization's senior leadership tear it apart when one person was given front page newsletter recognition while others were relegated to the last page. It didn't matter that the newsletter was between editors and no one thought to explain how they had handled retirement stories in the past so have a carefully considered plan on how you will recognize, and honor, those who are leaving.
- Remember to share it with bee club leadership so they approve of the plan, know what to expect and give them the option to opt out. And then **honor their wishes.**
- If you decide to do something contrary to what they have expressed, discuss it with a spouse or family member first and **enlist them** to help you. They should know whether the gesture will be well accepted or not. If it backfires, then the bee club has an accomplice who can soften the reaction.
- The bottom line is you want people to leave **on good terms.**

THANKING PEOPLE

Just as people have been thanked all along, they should also be **thanked as you leave.**

One of the nicest gifts I received from a departing president was a card with a "one free call" inside. The note thanked me for all of my help and said whenever I found myself in a corner to feel free to call him. I still have that card in my jewelry box.

If you have regular habits, such as having a cup of coffee together, or imbibing a beer, pay for a round. The thank you does not need to be formal or complicated; it just needs to **be well placed.**

If you write a parting letter in your newsletter and start listing names, be very careful **not to leave anyone out.** Some people get upset by being overlooked or excluded so if in doubt, leave them all out.

If you keep your focus on the incoming team and wishing them well, you can hand off the baton with a positive message.

Working with other beekeepers can be fun, in and out of club meetings. Gregg Hitchings, center, used my bee buddy David Draker and I as his guinea pigs fall of 2019 for some of the Great Plains Master Beekeeping-related testing he developed for Missouri's master beekeeping program. Gregg is a University of Florida certified master beekeeper and the chair of our state association's education committee. He has also been a regular impromptu visitor to our club meetings.. When he does, we gladly throw our meeting agenda out the window to spend time with him. Thanks for stopping by, Gregg! And ladies no, there is no such thing as a good hair day in real beekeeping.

SO AGAIN, WHY START A BEE CLUB?

I know, all you really want to do is play with honey bees. Or talk about bees, or better yet, talk about playing with bees. I get it, I am a founder of a local bee club and I still have friends who like to remind me I am now retired so why do I do this?

The bottom line is that you as the founder, and in leadership, will also benefit from the community you create. The planning and work that takes place between meetings adds value, from learning new information and concepts to being fun, which then translates to better meetings. Then there is the added bonus of lending each other a hand when we need it in the bee yard and, if you are lucky, making lifelong friends.

In addition to enjoying seeing other beekeepers be successful, the bee club also gives you an **opportunity to continue to learn.** Beekeepers with a range of experience flow in and out of our bee club meetings, sharing stories and experience as well as observations. Since beekeeping is quite local, having a platform to share local conditions will contribute to everyone's success.

In the end, do it because of the bees, both honey bees and native bees. They are fascinating, transformative and essential to our quality of life. As I said in my April 2019 TEDx talk "Why Bugs Matter," they are the "foundation of our interdependent ecosystems, the small overlooked creatures that run our world." Here is a link to the entire presentation: https://bit.ly/WhyBugsMatter

I can't think of a better reason to shuffle some paper, **can you?**

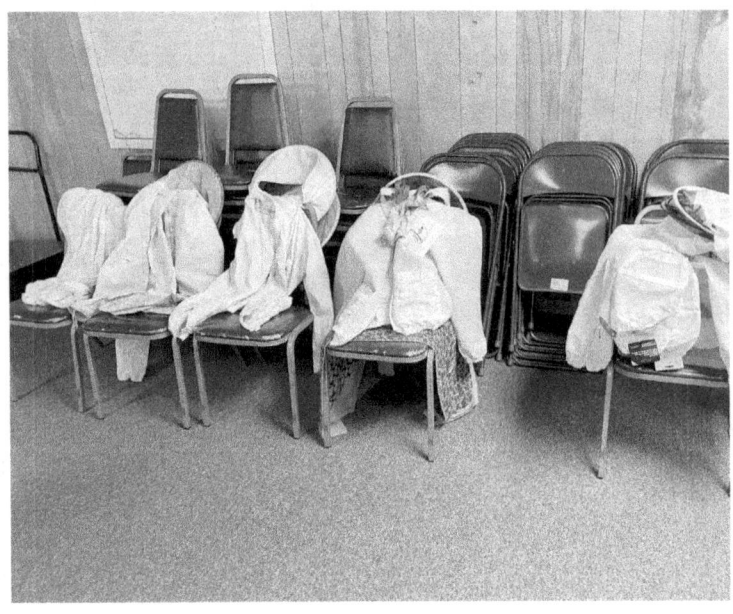

*Looks like beekeepers falling asleep in back of the room, doesn't it? These are bee suits we periodically bring into club meetings so new beekeepers can determine the best sizing. Don't leave your club like these empty bee suits; **make sure you are leaving a good structure** behind for the next club leaders.*

HONEY LEMON CAKE RECIPE

(With thanks to Gina Draker for sharing!)

9" round cake

Ingredients

Cake

- 1 ½ cups (180g) Cake Flour
- ¾ cup (72g) almond flour (I'm guessing you could substitute any other flour here).
- 1 ½ teaspoons baking powder
- ½ teaspoon baking soda
- ½ teaspoon salt
- 8 tablespoons (113g) unsalted butter, at room temperature
- ½ cup (99g) sugar (I used caster sugar)
- 2 large eggs, at room temperature
- ¼ cup (85g) honey
- zest (grated rind) of 1 lemon (I substituted a 1/2 tsp lemon oil - because I had it in my pantry)
- 1 teaspoon vanilla extract
- ½ teaspoon lemon extract (I substituted 1 tsp lemon powder - did not have extract)
- 1 cup (227g) buttermilk or plain yogurt, at room temperature (I used full fat Greek yogurt and stirred in a tbsp buttermilk powder).

*When safe, invite club members to **share favorite treats**. Doesn't this look delicious? It is a honey lemon cake made with delightful bee-related cake forms. You're welcome.*

Glaze

- ¼ cup (85g) honey
- 2 tablespoons (28g) unsalted butter, cold
- 1 tablespoon lemon juice

Instructions:

1. Preheat the oven to 350°F. Grease a honeycomb pan or 9" round cake pan.

2. To make the batter: Weigh the flours, or measure them by gently spooning them into a measuring cup and sweeping off the excess. In a medium bowl, whisk together the flours, baking powder, baking soda, and salt.

3. In a large mixing bowl, beat together the butter and sugar until light and fluffy.

4. Add the eggs one at a time, beating for a minute or two and scraping the sides and bottom of the bowl between additions. Beat in the honey, zest, and extracts.

5. Stir in the flour mixture in three additions, alternating with the buttermilk or yogurt, beginning and ending with the flour mixture.

6. Spread the batter into the prepared pan; if you're baking in the honeycomb pan, we recommend tapping the pan firmly on the counter to help eliminate any air bubbles at the bottom.

7. Bake the cake for 30 to 35 minutes, until it's a deep golden brown and a cake tester inserted into the center comes out clean.

8. Remove the cake from the oven, allow it to cool in the pan for 10 minutes, then turn it out onto a rack.

9. To make the glaze: Combine the honey, butter, and lemon juice in a microwave-safe bowl or in a small saucepan set over medium-low heat. Heat until the butter is melted and stir until smooth.

10. Brush the glaze onto the warm cake. Allow the cake to cool completely before cutting.

11. Store leftover cake, well wrapped, at room temperature for several days. Freeze for longer storage.

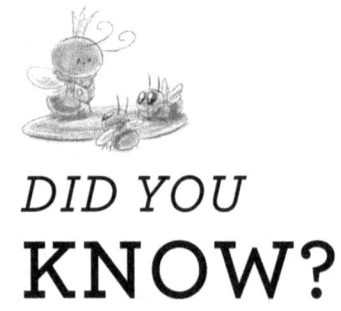

DID YOU KNOW?

- Honey bees visit 40,000 flowers to make one teaspoon of honey.
- It takes me about 8 hours monthly to prepare for a bee club meeting.
- My first jar of honey cost an estimated $889.52 not counting taxes.

(Courtesy of "my math.")

CHAPTER 16

Bee Club References

"Listen to the bees and let them guide you."
— *Brother Adam, (1898-1996) A Benedictine monk, beekeeper and authority on bee breeding, he developed the Buckfast bee. Birth name Karl Kerle.*

There are a number of resources available to help you. If you are working with an existing bee club, make sure to get a **copy of the existing Bylaws and Articles of Incorporation.** I was surprised to hear from a number of existing club leaders who didn't know they had these documents or couldn't find copies. When all else fails, if you are formally incorporated, your Secretary of State and/or Attorney General's offices should have a formal copy.

Regardless of your status, you're starting a new club or revitalizing an existing one, your best friends will be **an accountant and a lawyer.** Don't copy something as is and just change the name, or take any formal legal steps without getting professional advice. It can—no, it will save you a lot of grief later. Bottom line is do it right the first time.

The following are some frequently-asked questions I've been asked since the first edition of this book. I asked Michele Colopy, executive director of LEAD for Pollinators, Inc. for her advice on some of these questions since her nonprofit

*Provide good reference books and **take a lot of photos** from different angles. Can you believe I didn't notice those torn shades when I took this photo? It's easy to overlook the obvious!*

organization is focused on helping beekeepers with everything from leadership, education, action to development. She also has an excellent blog that also addresses similar issues at https://leadforpollinators.org/our-blog/

FREQUENTLY-ASKED QUESTIONS

1. *I want to accept donations for our club through Facebook but Facebook won't let me. What do I have to do?*

    Facebook requires you to be a formally registered 501©3 charitable nonprofit before you can accept donations through Facebook. To receive donations from Facebook, you will be asked for copies of all of your legal documents, a designated club representative so appointed by a vote of your board, and your registration with the Network for Good, the entity that issues the donation checks to your organization.

2. *Can I set up a "GoFundMe ©"page to collect club donations?*

    Donations made to personal GoFundMe© fundraisers are generally considered to be "personal gifts." For the most part, those are not taxed as income in the US. These donations are not tax deductible for donors. There may be cases where the income is taxable for organizers. For example, if the donations are considered income for your club. As part of GoFundMe©'s Terms and Conditions, you have represented that you are not providing any goods or services in exchange for the donation of funds. As a result, GoFundMe© will not provide any tax documentation for money raised, nor will GoFundMe© report the funds collected as earned income. Be sure to read the terms and conditions of any online fundraising platform you may use for tax responsibilities. To make sure that you are complying with tax laws, consult with a tax professional before you set up the account and keep good donation records.

3. *We have some young club members who refuse to come into our meetings until after we hold our club prayer. Should our bee club offer a prayer?*

    If your club is associated with a religious organization, the prayer may be consistent with the association your club has with that organization. If the club is not associated with a religious organization, then a prayer should not be offered. Most clubs want to be inclusive and welcome everyone. If your club has a non-discriminatory policy, then you also do not want to favor one "creed" over another one, you could be in violation of your own non-discrimination policy.

4. *I can't get anyone to step up and volunteer so our club may go defunct. What can I do?*

   Sometimes people don't know how to help so start with a list of the basic things your club needs to do to continue. Share it with your executive committee and/or board and ask for volunteers. For club positions, write up descriptions of what those jobs involve and ask for "temporary" volunteers to fill in. Sometimes once people get involved, they are willing to continue. Even if they don't, the temporary fills will buy you time to find others who may be interested.

   You may need to hold a planning session with your Board and interested members to determine if the mission and focus of the organization is still current. Revising the reason for the organization can help to revitalize the organization. Groups such as your State Association or Nonprofits or LEAD for Pollinators, Inc. can assist you in reviewing and revitalizing your organization.

5. *One of our (volunteer) officers is not doing their job. How do we get them to do their job?*

   Do all of your officers have a list of what they should be doing in their jobs? Job descriptions are often overlooked but are very important when running a club with volunteers. If you don't have job descriptions, develop them for your executive committee as a whole, not pinpointing just one person. That way everyone is clear about who is doing what job. Then extend that to your board of directors if you have one, and your committee chairs. Frankly people will tend to volunteer more if they know what is expected of them so this should help you with recruiting, too.

6. *Our club leaders are burned out. How can I get them re-engaged?*

   Burnout happens a little too frequently because there is a tendency to keep going back to those good, reliable volunteers.

   Make a list of your club must dos and nice to dos. Share the must do list with club members and ask if there are volunteers to tackle those particular items. Have the new volunteers work with existing club leadership to take on some of those responsibilities. And don't take on anything more until you have your club basics first covered. If some nice to dos fall off your schedule, that's one of the consequences of not having enough volunteers. Sometimes cancelling a favorite club activity will emphasize the need for more volunteers.

You may also need to get your Board together to agree on what gets dropped and what you can continue doing. For some people having their current overworked condition recognized is a step in the right direction, especially if they see that the club is trying to do something about it. Don't ignore signs of burnout, it can back fire on your club and have long term consequences.

7. *I volunteered to help our club with this particular event and now they assume I will continue to do it forever. How do I get out of this situation gracefully?*

First identify who you have helping you who may be interested in taking over. Talk to them about it and decide on a time frame for passing on the torch. If you don't have any prospective candidates, tell your club Board when you plan to step down. Give them time to locate someone and volunteer to help train then. Stick to your exit date, though, or the Board may be tempted not to take your retirement from this position seriously.

If there is something else you are interested in doing, see if that person would be interested in trading with you. Sometimes people don't think about opportunities if someone is filing a particular position.

8. *I am a club Board member and would like to sell honey to my club to raise funds. We voted at our last Board meeting to do so. Now I am being told by another honey producer that my selling my honey to the club is a conflict of interest and he wants the Board to buy his honey. How do I get my club to buy my honey?*

Being a voting Board member and voting to buy your own honey is self-dealing and a conflict of interest. For future reference, your Board should have a written policy about how they plan to do business with Board members to clearly outline how they can fairly do business with Board members. In addition, you should not have voted on the proposal to buy your honey.

Going forward, your club could outline a proposal of what they need, share it with all club members and set a deadline to get proposals. Once all proposals are in, a committee could review the proposals and make a Board recommendation. At that time you should step aside from any discussion or voting. Hopefully you have also volunteered time to help the club so your club association is not just so that you can personally benefit from honey sales.

9. *Our club wants to start a juvenile beekeeping program. Where do we start?*

    Contact your local University Extension office and find out what current programs they have for children and young people ages 18 and below. In many cases, an existing program such as 4-H, a youth development program, will be glad to work with you to provide positive, hands-on, fun and educational opportunities. The advantage of working with this and other similar programs is that they already have the administrative support in place so your club can focus on primarily the beekeeping side.

    Understand that most under age programs require participant background checks and parental permission. There may also be some restrictions on using under aged photos so check before taking photos.

10. *Why do you use funny book cover cartoons? I love them but they are so different than other beekeeping books.*

    They are different and that's the point, the three beekeeping reference books in this series are unique. The covers had to be eye catching and reflect that you would not find some of this information in any other books. My illustrator also captured my personal fun and whimsical aesthetic; I am a true believer that we should all spend time with, and on, what is fun and gives us joy. Did you notice how many times I am wearing a bee headband in photos?

    When I tested the three book covers with potential buyers, people said the book covers not only caught their eye and prompted them to pick them up but they made them smile. Being eye-catching is a major step with a new book; prompting someone to pick it up is a huge second step. But make someone smile looking at a management book? Not many other management books can make that claim!

    If you have a question, email me at 4charlottewiggins@gmail.com. I look forward to hearing from you!

RESOURCES FOR CLUB MANAGEMENT, ORGANIZATION AND FUNDRAISING

CHARITY LAWYER BLOG

- https://charitylawyerblog.com

IRS CHARITIES AND NONPROFIT RULES:

- https://www.irs.gov/charities-non-profits/charitable-organizations

IRS TAX ID APPLICATION ONLINE

- https://www.irs-ein-tax-id-number.com/nonprofit.aspx

LEAD FOR POLLINATORS, INC. (LEADERSHIP, EDUCATION, ACTION, DEVELOPMENT)

- Michele Colopy, Executive Director, Master's degree in Nonprofit Management: info@leadforpollinators.org
- www.leadforpollinators.org
- Blog: https://leadforpollinators.org/our-blog

MEETING MANAGEMENT:

- Ignore Robert's Rules Thing: https://bit.ly/BCB-Roberts-Rules
- Law of Order: Key Terms: https://bit.ly/KeyTerms-LOO
- Beginner's Guide to Governing Documents: https://bit.ly/LOO-docs
- Going for Consensus, Not Robert's Rules: https://bit.ly/NotRobertsRules
- Martha's Rules of Order: https://bit.ly/MarthasROO

- Robert's Rules of Order Online: http://www.rulesonline.com
- **National Council of Nonprofits** has affiliates in each state
- https://www.councilofnonprofits.org
- **Network for Good:** https://www.networkforgood.com

STATE LEGAL FILINGS, REGISTRATION, STATUTORY AGENTS, & INSTRUCTIONAL GUIDES FOR NONPROFITS:

- Secretary of State in each of the 50 states
- Attorney General in each of the 50 states
- Charitable Board Member Guidelines published by each State's Attorney General, Secretary of State, or Consumer Affairs Office

BEE CLUB HELPFUL REFERENCES

There are a number of available **free resources** you can tap. The ones listed here are ones I have used with our bee club and found useful with this book. None of them have paid me to have them listed.

Make sure the sources you use and post are **appropriate to your bee club's location.** Taping a website in Florida will not have a lot of information appropriate to your beekeeping so make sure you are **looking at appropriate references** to your area.

- American Bee Journal: https://www.americanbeejournal.com
- American Beekeeping Federation: www.abfnet.org
- Apimondia: www.apimondia.com/en
- Bee and Butterfly Habitat Fund: https://beeandbutterflyfund.org
- Bees and Wasps Guide: https://extension2.missouri.edu/G7391
- Bee Culture Magazine: www.beeculture.com
- Bee Informed Partnership: https://beeinformed.org
- Bee Research Lab/Beltsville, Maryland (free bee testing): https://bit.ly/FreeBeeTest
- Beepods.com: https://bit.ly/beepods

- Eastern Apicultural Society: https://www.easternapiculture.org
- Entomological Society of America: https://www.entsoc.org
- Facebook Community Standards: https://www.facebook.com/communitystandards/
- Generate Your Own Queen Rearing Calendar: www.thebeeyard.org/queen-rearing-calendar/
- Heartland Apicultural Society, the Midwest's annual beekeeping conference: http://www.heartlandbees.org
- Heroes to Hives (Military Veterans): https://bit.ly/HeroesHives
- Honeybee Health Coalition Tools for *Varroa* Management:
- https://honeybeehealthcoalition.org/varroa/
- Keeping Your Bees Safe from *Varroa* by Meghan Milbrath: https://bit.ly/VarroaByMeghan
- Missouri S&T TEDx "Why Bugs Matter": https://bit.ly/WhyBugsMatter
- National Honey Board (yumm, recipes): https://www.honey.com
- National Honey Board Honey Beer Competition (who knew?): http://honeybeercompetition.com
- Ohio State University Bee Lab Webinars: http://u.osu.edu/beelab/courses/
- The Bee MD: http://www.thebeemd.com
- Western Apicultural Society: https://westernapiculturalsociety.org
- Wikipedia: https://en.wikipedia.org
- World Bee Day Sponsor: https://www.un.org/en/observances/bee-day

- Other: _____

_____

Your Notes

Your Notes

_____

_____

_____

_____

_____

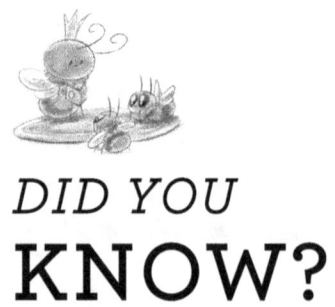

DID YOU KNOW?

- The darker the honey, the greater amount of antioxidant properties it has.
- The first Anglo-Saxons drank beer made from water and honeycomb, with herbs for flavoring.
- The word "honeymoon" is derived from the ancient tradition of supplying a newlywed couple with a month's supply of mead in order to ensure happiness and fertility.

(Courtesy of Beepods.com)

CHAPTER 17

Sample Check Lists and Documents

"He is not worthy of the honey-comb That shuns the hives because the bees have stings."
—William Shakespeare
(1564–1616) English playwright, poet and actor

To help you save time, and money, the following are most of the sample check lists and documents included in earlier chapters. I didn't include some of the basic samples such as thank you notes, you can refer back to those as necessary.

<u>While I hold the copyright and all rights to these materials,</u> **I hereby give you my permission to reproduce and use the following information ONLY to establish, and manage, a bee club.** In other words, feel free to copy this section and share with your planning team so you can all use them as guides as you plan your club and related activities. *Do NOT copy verbatim; check with your Secretary of State, Attorney General, local accountant and attorney before finalizing anything. Promise?*

When you pull the check lists and samples together, you will start to develop a skeleton for your club. Check with a local attorney and accountant to make sure you are headed in the right direction. **The key ingredients are to attract active volunteers and have coffee.** *Don't forget to have fun!*

1. Sample Annual Volunteer Code of Conduct
2. Sample Articles of Incorporation
3. Sample Bee Club Goals
4. Sample Bee Club Meeting Notices
5. Sample Beginning Beekeeping Class Agenda
6. Sample Beginning Beekeeping Class Survey
7. Sample Bylaws
8. Sample Class Survey
9. Sample Club Charter Agreement
10. Sample Code of Conduct
11. Sample Cover Coloring Page
12. Sample Expense Estimates
13. Sample Gift Certificate
14. Sample Meeting Agenda
15. Sample Meeting Notice
16. Sample Meeting Room Comparison Check List
17. Sample Memorandum of Understanding
18. Sample Minor Photo Release Form
19. Sample Monthly Club Programs
20. Sample Monthly Meeting Calendar
21. Sample Photo Release Form
22. Sample Planning Goals
23. Sample News Release
24. Sample Newsletter Guidelines
25. Sample Officer Job Descriptions
26. Sample Sign Up Sheet
27. Sample Volunteer Jobs Check List

SAMPLE VOLUNTEER ANNUAL CODE OF CONDUCT

Volunteers are key partners, helping guide and deliver programs that matter to (state) citizens. The university depends and expects all volunteers to understand and uphold the following Volunteer Code of Conduct at all times while serving as a volunteer.

BE ACCOUNTABLE TO AND WORK WITHIN THE UNIVERSITY SYSTEM

1. Work within the scope of assigned volunteer role and follow all related program policies and procedures.

2. Conduct behavior in strict accordance with applicable laws and confidential information policies, using confidential information only as needed to perform volunteer duties. The following rules apply:

    a. access confidential information only with proper approval and refrain from misusing or treating it carelessly;

    b. do not divulge, copy, release, sell, loan, review, alter or destroy any confidential information except as properly authorized;

    c. understand and agree that any violation of the responsibilities explained in this section subjects a volunteer to discipline, possible removal from the volunteer role or legal liability.

What is meant by confidentiality? Confidential information means personal information of another person, which includes home addresses, telephone numbers, social security numbers, birth dates, etc. Also, do not include personal contact information of another in newsletters and announcements without their expressed consent.

3. Treat all youth and adults equally, without discrimination. This includes providing equal access to participation for all youth and adults, regardless of race, color, sex, pregnancy, national origin, ancestry, sexual orientation, gender identity, gender expression, religion, age, veteran status, disability, or any other status protected by applicable federal or state law. Sexual violence is also

prohibited, including but not limited to sexual misconduct, sexual exploitation, sex-based stalking, and dating/intimate partner violence.

4. Avoid harming youth or adults, whether through sexual harassment, physical force, verbal or mental abuse or neglect. Retaliation for making or supporting a report of discrimination or harassment is also prohibited.

5. If your volunteer responsibilities meet the definition of a mandated reporter (i.e. anyone with care, custody or control of a child), then assume the role of a mandated reporter and, if concerned a child has been/or will be abused and/or neglected, contact the child abuse hotline. If it appears the child is in imminent danger, contact law enforcement as well.

When am "I" a Mandated Reporter? If youth are registered participants in a program, you are responsible to report suspected symptoms of child abuse and neglect even if parents are present. Exception: When a school visits, the teacher in charge of the group is the mandated reporter.

6. Avoid conflict of interest between assigned volunteer role(s) and personal business interests.

BE A POSITIVE ROLE MODEL AT ALL TIMES

1. Obey all laws of the locality, state and nation, including laws against forgery, theft, destruction or defacement of property.

2. Display mutual respect to others, practicing patience, cooperation and teamwork.

3. Practice personal and intellectual integrity.

4. Under no circumstances engage in unlawful manufacture, distribution, dispensation, possession, or use of a controlled substance at any club event. Avoid unlawful possession, use and/or distribution of alcohol at any club event. Avoid misuse or abuse of prescribed or over-the-counter drugs.

5. Be respectful of diverse opinions and perspectives.

6. Actively promote a safe environment for participants, volunteers, visitors, staff and others involved in the program.

Please consider volunteering as a privilege, not a right. Adhering to the code of conduct ensures the safety and protection of all, including yourself. Additionally, you have the authority to report abuses of the code of conduct to your supervisor. Failure to uphold any of the code of conduct standards above may result in coaching by a supervisor. Depending on the severity, this may include reassignment, role restriction and, if appropriate, removal from all volunteer roles. As representatives of the club, we have a shared responsibility to watch out for one another and to ensure the code of conduct is being followed.

END OF SAMPLE VOLUNTEER ANNUAL CODE OF CONDUCT

Your Notes

SAMPLE BEE CLUB NONPROFIT ARTICLES OF INCORPORATION

The undersigned natural person(s) of the age of eighteen years of age for the purpose of forming a corporation under the Missouri Nonprofit Corporation Law adopt the following Articles of Incorporation:

7. The name of the corporation is Sample Bee Club, Inc.

8. The corporation is a Public Benefit Corporation.

9. The period of duration of the corporation is perpetual. The name and street address of the Registered Agent and the Registered Office is Sample Club Organizer, Sample Lane, Sample, MO. 00000. (The registered agent or statutory agent should be the current treasurer. Ensure this agent is updated as needed. The club should also determine if it wants to use a post office box for the main address so that mail doesn't end up lost at a personal address as officers change.)

10. The name and address of the incorporator is Sample, 00 Sample Lane, Sample, Mo. 00000.

11. The corporation shall not have any members.

12. The corporation is formed for the following purposes:

    d. The corporation is organized exclusively for charitable, religious, educational and scientific purposes, including, for such purposes, the making of distributions to organizations that qualify as exempt organizations under section 501(c)(3) of the Internal Revenue Code, or the corresponding section of any future federal tax code.

    e. By way of qualification, it is hereby further provided that: (1) No part of the net earnings of the corporation shall inure to the benefit of, or be distributable to is members, trustees, officers or other private persons, except that the corporation shall be authorized and empowered to pay reasonable compensation for services rendered and to make payments and distributions in furtherance of the purposes set forth herein. (2) No substantial part of the activities of the corporation shall be the carrying on of propaganda, or otherwise attempting to influence legislation, and the corporation shall not participate in, or intervene in (including the publishing or distribution of statements) any political campaign on behalf of or in opposition to any candidate for public office.

13. Notwithstanding any other provision of these Articles, the corporation shall not carry on any other activities not permitted to be carried on

    a. by a corporation exempt from federal income tax under section 501(c)(3) of the Internal Revenue code, or the corresponding section of any future federal tax code, or

    b. by a corporation, contributions to which are deductible under section 170(c)(2) of the Internal Revenue Code, of the corresponding section of any future federal tax code.

14. Upon the dissolution of the corporation, assets shall be distributed for one of more exempt purposes within the meaning of section 501(c)(3) of the Internal Revenue Code, or the corresponding section of any future federal tax code, or shall be distributed to the federal government, or to a state or local government, for a public purpose. Any such assets not so disposed of shall be disposed of by the Circuit Court of (local county, state) or some other Court of competent jurisdiction of the county in which the principal office of the corporation is then located, exclusively for such purposes or to such organization or organizations, as said Court shall determine, which are organized and operated exclusively for such purposes.

    c. To exercise all rights and powers conferred upon it by the provisions of the laws of (your resident state) generally pertaining to nonprofit corporations, including, without limiting the generality of any of the foregoing to acquire by bequest, devise, gift, purchase, lease or otherwise, either absolutely or in trust, any property of any sort or nature without limitation as to its amount of value, and to hold, invest, reinvest, manage, use, apply, employ, sell, expend, disperse, lease, mortgage, convey, donate or otherwise dispose of such property, and the income, principal and proceeds thereof, for any of the purposes herein set forth.

15. The effective date of this document is the date it is filed by the Secretary of State of (your state).

The undersigned swears that the matters set forth in the foregoing petition are true and correct according to their best knowledge, information and belief, subject to the penalties of making a false affidavit or declaration.

IN AFFIRMATION THEREOF, the facts stated above are true and correct according to the best knowledge, information and belief of the undersigned, subject to the penalties provided under (your state statutes)

(Signed by the incorporator)

Your Notes

_____

_____

_____

_____

_____

_____

_____

SAMPLE BEE CLUB GOALS

WHAT YOU WANT TO DO, HOW DO YOU PLAN TO DO IT

	GOAL 1	GOAL 2	GOAL 3	NOTES
Describe goals				
How to implement				
What action				
Why desired result(s)?				
By whom (name) someone responsible				
What needed (list supplies/actions)				
By when (set a goal date)				
What happens if goal not met (describe impact)				
Other needed measurable steps				

SAMPLE BEE CLUB MEETING NOTICES

This is how information can be pulled together for a community calendar notice:

1. The Eldon Bee Club will meet Saturday, January 1, 2019 at the Community Center from 2 – 4 p.m. Everyone is welcome. For more details, email ***bees@gmail.com and call (000) 000-0000.

Or

2. The Eldon Bee Club will meet Saturday, January 1, 2019 at the Community Center from 2-4 p.m. The agenda includes how to winter feed bees. Volunteers are welcome to discuss fundraising ideas. No dues. (Or donations appreciated) Refreshments will be available. For further information, visit eldonbeeclub.com, email ***bees@gmail.com and call (000) 000-0000.

Your Notes

_____

_____

_____

_____

_____

SAMPLE BEGINNING CLASS AGENDA

9 a.m. – 9:15 a.m.	Welcome/intros
9:15 a.m. – 10:15 am	Why Do You Want to Keep Bees?
	What Is Pollination
	History of Beekeeping
	Bee Biology
10:15 a.m. – 10:30 a.m.	*Break*
10:30 a.m. – 11:30 a.m.	How to Get Bees
	Cost of Beekeeping
	Hive Options
	Starting Equipment
	Parts of a Hive
11:30 a.m. – 12:30 p.m.	*Lunch*
12:30 p.m. – 1:30 p.m.	Make Your Own Hives
1:30 p.m. – 1:45 p.m.	How to Install Packages
1:45 p.m. – 2:45 p.m.	*Break*
	Pests and Diseases
	How to Inspect Hives
2:45 p.m. – 3 p.m.	Beekeeper's Yearly Task Calendar
3 p.m. – 3:45 p.m.	*Break*
3:45 p.m. – 4 p.m.	Questions and Answers
	Bee Buddies & Mentoring
	Class survey
	Wrap Up

SAMPLE BEGINNING CLASS SURVEY

Beginning Beekeeping Class Survey Date:_____

What did you think of the class? Please place a mark in the box that best reflects your answers and add comments for more details so we can make appropriate adjustments. Thank you!

QUESTIONS	5 GREAT	4 GOOD	3 OK	2 FAIR	1 POOR	COMMENTS
Did the class meet your expectations?						
Did you like the room?						
How were class materials?						
How could this class have been better?						
What other class topics would you be interested in?						
Any other comments?						

Your Name	Email	Phone Number	Hometown

SAMPLE BYLAWS

ARTICLE I – PURPOSES AND RESTRICTIONS

The purposes of the Corporation shall be those nonprofit purposes stated in the Articles of Incorporation, as they may be amended. By way of qualification, it is hereby further provided that:

- A. No part of the net earnings of the Corporation shall inure to the benefit of, or be distributable to its members, trustees, officers, or other private persons, except that the Corporation shall be authorized and empowered to pay reasonable compensation for services rendered and to make payments and distributions in furtherance of the purposes set forth in the Articles of Incorporation.

- B. No substantial part of the Corporation activities shall be the carrying on of propaganda, or otherwise attempting to influence legislation, and the Corporation shall not participate in, or intervene in (including the publishing or distribution of statements) any political campaign on behalf of or in opposition to any candidate for public office.

- C. Notwithstanding any other provision of these By-Laws or Articles of Incorporation, the Corporation shall not carry on any other activities not permitted to be carried on:

    - a. by a corporation exempt from federal income tax under section 501(c)(3) of the Internal Revenue Code, or the corresponding section of any future federal tax code, or

    - b. by a corporation, contributions to which are deductible under section 170 (c)(2) of the Internal Revenue Code, or the corresponding section of any future federal tax code.

- D. To exercise all rights and powers conferred upon it by the provisions of (cite state laws) generally pertaining to nonprofit corporations, including, without limiting the generality of any of the foregoing to acquire by bequest, devise, gift, purchase, lease of otherwise, either absolutely or in trust, any property of any sort or nature without limitation as to is amount of value, and to hold, invest, reinvest, manage, use, apply, employ, sell, expend, disperse, lease, mortgage, convey, donate or otherwise dispose of such property, and the income, principal and proceeds thereof, for any of the purposes herein set forth.

ARTICLE II – OFFICES

The principal office of the Corporation in the (name the state) shall be located in the (name of city). The Corporation may have such other offices within or without said City as may be required.

The registered office of the Corporation required under the laws of the (name state) to be maintained in the (name of state) may be, but not need be, identical with the principal office in the (name of state) and the address of the registered office may be changed from time to time in conformity with the laws of (name of state). The Corporation shall maintain a registered agent whose address shall be the same as that of the registered Corporation office.

ARTICLE III – MEMBERS

The Corporation shall not have shareholders or members.

ARTICLE IV – BOARD OF DIRECTORS

A. **Management.** Corporation affairs shall be managed, supervised and controlled by a self-perpetuating Board of Directors consisting of not less than THREE (3) persons and not more than SEVEN (7) persons elected by a majority of the Board in a manner specified in paragraph B herein below. ONE (1) of the initial directors shall serve a one (1) year term; ONE (1) of the initial directors shall serve a two (2) year term: and ONE (1) of the initial directors shall serve a THREE (3) year term.

B. **Term and Election of Directors.** The full term of office of directors shall be THREE (3) years, and to the extent practicable taking into account increases or decreases in the number of directors constituting the Board of Directors, one-third (1/3) of the Board of Directors shall be elected each year at the annual meeting of the Board of Directors, the directors so elected filing the place of retiring directors. In the event of a change in the number of directors, the resolution effectuating such change shall specify the years in which the terms of the directorships thereby created shall first expire. Vacancies occurring in the Board of Directors, including vacancies due to an increase in the number of directors, may be filled by the directors then in office. Any director may serve an indefinite number of terms.

C. **Removal and Resignation.** Any director may resign at any time by giving written notice to the Board of Directors, the President of the Corporation and/or Secretary; unless otherwise specified therein, the acceptance off such resignation shall not be necessary to make it effective. Any director may be removed, with or without cause, by the affirmative vote of a majority of the Board of Directors at a meeting of the Directors at which a quorum is present; provided, however, that a director may be removed only at a meeting called for the purpose of removing the Director, and the notice of such meeting shall state the purpose, or one of the purposes, is the Director removal. Any such resignation of removal shall take effect at the time specified therein.

D. **Annual Meetings.** The annual meeting of the Board of Directors shall be held in the month of January of each year, and shall be held for the purpose of electing new board members, electing new officers and transacting such other business as may come before the meeting.

E. **Special Meetings.** Special Board of Directors meetings may be called by or at the request of the President or by any two directors.

F. **Meetings.** Board of Directors meetings, regular or special, may be held at any place either within (name the state), or from time to time by resolution of the Board of Directors or by unanimous written consent of the members thereof. Board of Directors meetings shall be held upon such notice as provided herein. Neither the business to be transacted at, nor the purpose of, any regular or special Board of Directors meeting need be specified in the notice of waiver of notice of such meeting.

G. **Participation Through Electronic Communication.** Board of Directors members, or of any Board of Directors-designated committees, may participate in a Board of Directors meeting of Board of Directors committee meeting by means of conference telephone or similar communications equipment whereby all persons participating can hear each other, and participation in a meeting in this manner shall constitute presence in person at the meeting.

H. **Action Without Meeting.** Any action which is required to be or may be taken at a Board of Directors meeting, or a Board of Directors Committee meeting, may be taken without a meeting if consents in writing, settling forth the action so taken, are signed by all Board of Directors members or of the committee as the case may be. The consent shall have the same force and effect as a unanimous vote at the meeting duly held, and may be stated as such in any certificate of document. The Secretary shall file the consents with the Board of Directors meeting minutes or of the committee meeting minutes as the case may be.

I. **Notice.** Notice of any annual, regular or special meeting shall be given at least FIVE (5) days previous thereto by written notice delivered either personally, by facsimile, electronic mail, or other form of wire or wireless communication, or by mail to each Director at his or her business or home address. Written notice shall be deemed effective at the earlier of the following: (1) When received; (2) file days after its deposit in the US mail, as evidenced by the postmark, if mailed correctly and with first class postage affixed; or (3) on the date shown on the return receipt, if sent by registered or certified mail, return receipt requested, and the receipt is signed by or on behalf of the addressee. Any Director may waive notice of any meeting. The attendance of a director at any meeting shall constitute a waiver of notice of such meeting, except where a Director attends a meeting for the express purpose of objecting to the transaction of any business because the meeting is not lawfully called or convened. Neither the business to be transacted at, nor the purpose of, any regular or special Board of Directors meeting need be specified in the notice or waiver of notice of such meeting.

J. **Voting.** Each Director shall be entitled to one (1) vote on each matter submitted to a Board of Directors vote. A vote of a majority of the votes entitled to be cast by the Directors present at a meeting at which a quorum is present shall be necessary for the adoption of any matter voted upon by the Board of Directors.

K. **Quorum.** A Board of Directors majority shall constitute a quorum for the transaction of business at any Board of Directors meeting.

L. **Manner of Acting and Rules of Order.** In all matters not covered by the By-Laws, parliamentary procedures shall be governed by the manual knows as "Robert's Rules of Order, the Modern Edition." The act of the Board of Directors majority present at a Board of Directors meeting at which a quorum is present shall be the act of the Board of Directors, unless a greater number is required under the Articles of Incorporation, these By-Laws, any applicable (name of state) laws or Robert's Rules of Order.

M. **Number and Election.** The Corporation officers shall be a President, a Secretary/Treasurer. The Board of Directors may also elect a Vice President, Assistant Secretary and Assistant Treasurer. All officers shall be elected at the Board of Directors annual meeting by a majority of those Board members present, including newly-elected members, and said officers hall hold office at the pleasure of the Board of Directors until the next Annual meeting and until their successors shall have been elected and qualified. Where a vacancy occurs in an office, the Board of Directors shall fill the position for the unexpired term.

N. **President.** The President shall be the Corporation's chief executive officer. The President shall preside at all Board of Directors meetings and Board of Director Committee meetings and shall have the power to transact all of the usual, necessary and regular Corporation business as may be required and, with such prior Board authorization as may be required in these By-Laws to execute such contracts, deeds, bonds and other evidences of indebtedness, leases and other documents as shall be required by the Corporation; and, in general, shall perform all such other duties incident to the President's office and such other duties as the Board of Directors may prescribe from time to time.

O. **Secretary/Treasurer.** The Secretary/Treasurer shall record and preserve the Board of Directors and Committee meeting minutes, shall be responsible for authenticating Corporation records, shall cause notices of all Board of Directors meetings and committees to be given to the members thereof. Secretary/Treasurer shall be responsible for all Corporation funds shall direct that such funds be deposited in such bank or banks as Board of Directors may from time to time determine, and shall make reports to the Board of Directors as requested by the Board. The Secretary/Treasurer shall see that an accounting system is maintained in such a manner as to give a true and accurate accounting of the Corporation financial transactions, that reports of such transactions are presented promptly to the Board of Directors, that all expenditures are presented promptly to the Board of Directors, that all expenditures are made to the best possible advantage, and that all accounts payable are presented promptly for payment. The Secretary/Treasurer shall further perform such other duties incident to his or her office and as the Board of President may from time to time determine. If required by the Board of Directors, the Secretary/Treasurer shall give a bond for the faithful discharge of his or her duties in such sum and with such surety or sureties as the Board of Directors shall determine.

P. **Removal and Resignation.** Any officer may be removed, with or without cause, by the majority Board of Directors vote at any Board meeting. Any officer may resign at any time by giving written notice to the Board of Directors, the President or Secretary. Any such resignation or removal shall take effect at the time specified herein.

ARTICLE VI – GENERAL PROVISIONS

A. **Contracts, Etc. How Executed.** Except as in these Bylaws otherwise provided or restricted, the Board of Directors may authorize any officer or officers, agent or agents to enter into any contract or execute and deliver any instrument in the name of and on behalf of the Corp[oration, and such authority may be general or confined to specific instances; and, unless so authorized, no officer, agent or employee shall have any power or authority to bind the Corporation by any contract or engagement or to pledge its credit or to render it liable pecuniarily for any purpose or in any amount.

B. **Deposits.** All Corporation funds shall be deposited from time to time to the credit of the Corporation with such banks, bankers, trust companies or other depositories as the Board of Directors may select or as may be selected by any officer or officers, agent or agents of the Corporation to whom such power may be delegated from time to time by the Board of Directors.

C. **Checks, Drafts, etc.** All checks, drafts or other orders for the payment of money, notes, acceptances of other evidence of indebtedness issued in the name of the Corporation shall be signed by such officer of officers, agent or agents of the Corporation, and in such manner as shall be determined from time to time by Board of Directors resolution in accordance with the provisions of these Bylaws. Endorsements for deposit to the credit of the Corporation in any of its duly authorized depositories may be made without countersignature by the President or Secretary/Treasurer, or by any other officer of Corporation agent to whom the Board of Directors, by resolution, shall have delegated such power, or by hand-stamped impression in the name of the Directors.

ARTICLE VII – CONFLICT OF INTEREST

No contract or transaction between the Corporation and one or more of its Directors or officers, or between the Corporation and any other corporation, partnership, association, or organization in which one of more of its Directors or officers are Directors of officers, or have a financial interest, shall be void or voidable solely for that reason, or solely because the Director of officer is present at or participates in the meeting of the Board of committee thereof which authorizes the contract or transaction, or solely because his or her or their votes are counted for such purposes, if the material facts as to his or her relationship or interest and as to the contract or transaction are disclosed or are known to the Board of Directors or the committee, and the Board of committee in good faith, taking into account the fairness of the contract or transaction, authorizes the contract or transaction by the affirmative votes of a majority of the disinterested Directors present.

ARTICLE VIII – INDEMNIFICATION

A. **Mandatory indemnification.** The Corporation shall indemnify any Director who was wholly successful, on the merits or otherwise, in the defense of any proceeding to which the Director was a party because he or she is or was a Corporation Director against reasonable expenses actually incurred by the Director in connection with the proceeding.

B. **Permissive Indemnification.**

(1) The Corporation may indemnify any person who was or is a party or is threatened to be made a party to any threatened, pending or completed action, suit, or proceeding, whether civil, criminal, administrative or investigative, other than an action by or in the right of the Corporation, any reason of the fact that he or she is or was a Director, officer, employee

or agent of the Corporation, or is or was serving at the request of the Corporation, or is or was serving at the request of the corporation as a Director, officer, employee or agent of another corporation, partnership, joint venture, trust or other enterprise, against expenses, including attorney fees, judgments, fines and amounts paid in settlement actually and reasonably incurred by him or her in connection with such action, suit, or process if he or she acted in good faith and in a manner he or she reasonably believed to be in or not opposed to the Corporation's best interests, and, with respect to any criminal action or proceeding, had no reasonable cause to believe his or her conduct was unlawful. The termination of any action, suit, or proceeding by judgment, by order, by settlement, by conviction, or upon a plea of nolo contendere or its equivalent, shall not, or itself, create a presumption that the person did not act in good faith and in a manner which he or she reasonably believed to be in or not opposed to the Corporation's best interests and, with respect to any criminal action or proceeding, that the person had reasonable cause to believe that his or her conduct was unlawful.

(2) The Corporation may indemnify any person who was or is a party or is threatened to be made a party to any threatened, pending or completed action or suit by or in the right of the Corporation to procure a judgment in its favor by reason of the fact that he or she is or was a Director, officer, employee or agent of the Corporation, or is or was serving at the request of the Corporation as a Director, officer, employee or agent of another corporation, partnership, joint venture, trust or other enterprise against expenses, including attorney fees, and amounts paid in settlement actually and reasonably incurred by him or her in connection with the defense or settlement of the action or suit if he or she acted in good faith and in a manner he or she reasonably believed to be in or not opposed to the Corporation's best interests; except that no indemnification shall be made in respect of any claim, issue or matter as to which such person shall have been adjudged to be liable for negligence or misconduct in the performance of his or her duty to the Corporation unless and only to the extent that the court in which the action or suit was brought determines upon application that, despite the adjudication of liability and in view of all the circumstances of the case, the person is fairly and reasonably entitled to indemnification for such expenses for which the court shall deem proper.

(3) To the extent that a Director, officer, employee or agent of the Corporation has been successful on the merits or otherwise in defense of any action, suit, or proceeding referred to in subsections (1) and (2) of this section, or in defense of any claim, issue or matter therein, he or she shall be indemnified against expenses, including attorney fees, actually and reasonably incurred by him or her in connection with the action, suit or proceeding.

(4) Any indemnification under subsections (1) and (2) of this section, unless ordered by a court, shall be made by the Corporation only as authorized in the specific case upon a determination that indemnification of the Director, officer, employee or agent is proper in the circumstances because he or she has met the applicable standard of conduct set forth in this section. The determination shall be made by the Board of Directors by a majority vote of a quorum consisting of Directors who were not parties to the action, suit, or proceeding, or if such a quorum is not obtainable, or even if obtainable a quorum of disinterested Directors so directs, by independent legal counsel in a written opinion.

(5) Expenses incurred in defending a civil or criminal action, suit or proceeding may be paid by the Corporation in advance of the final disposition of the action, suit, or proceeding as authorized by the Board of Directors in the specific case upon receipt of an undertaking by or on behalf of the Director, officer, employee or agent to repay such amount unless is hall ultimately be determined that he or she is entitled to be indemnified by the Corporation as authorized in this section.

(6) The indemnification provided by this section shall not be deemed exclusive of any other rights to which those seeking indemnification may be entitled under (state statute), any other provision of law, the Articles of Incorporation of the Corporation of these Bylaws or any agreement, vote of disinterested Directors or otherwise, both as to action in his or her official capacity and as to action in another capacity while holding such office, and shall continue as to a person who has ceased to be a Director, officer, employee or agent and shall inure to the benefit of the heirs, executors and administrators of such a person.

(7) The Corporation shall have the power to give any further indemnity, in addition to the indemnity authorized or contemplated under other subsections of this section, including subsection (6), to any person

who is or was a Director, officer, employee or agent, or to any person who is or was serving at the request of the Corporation as a Director, officer, employee or agent of any other corporation, partnership, joint venture, trust or other enterprise, provided such further indemnity is either (i) authorized, directed or provided for in the Corporation Articles of Incorporation or any duly adopted amendment thereof, or (ii) is authorized, directed, or provided for in these Bylaws or agreement of the Corporation which has been adopted by a Board of Directors vote, and provided further that no such indemnity shall indemnify any person from or on account of such person's conduct which was finally adjudged to have been knowingly fraudulent, deliberately dishonest or willful misconduct.

(8) For the purpose of this section, references to the "Corporation" include all constituent corporations absorbed in a consolidation or merger as well as the resulting or surviving corporation so that any person who is or was a Director, officer, employee or agent of such a constituent corporation or is or was serving at the request of such constituent corporation as a Director, officer, employee or agent of another corporation, partnership, joint venture, trust or other enterprise shall stand in the same position under the provisions of this section with respect to the resulting or surviving corporation as he or she would if he or she had served the resulting or surviving corporation in the same capacity.

(9) For the purposes of this section, the term "other enterprise" shall include employee benefit plans; the term "fines" shall include any excise taxes assessed on a person with respect to an employee benefit plan; and the term "serving at the request of the Corporation" shall include any service as a Director, officer, employee or agent of the Corporation which imposes duties on, or involves services by, such Director, officer, employee, or agent with respect to an employee benefit plan, its participants, or beneficiaries; and a person who acted in good faith and in a manner he or she reasonably believed to be in the interest of the participants and beneficiaries of an employee benefit plan shall be deemed to have acted in a manner "not opposed to the best interests of the Corporation" as referred to in this section.

C. **Insurance.** The Corporation may purchase and maintain insurance on behalf of an individual who is or was a Director, officer, employee, or Corporation agent, or who, while a Director, officer, employee, or Corporation agent, is or was serving at the Corporation request as a Director, officer, partner, trustee, employee, or agent of another foreign or domestic business or nonprofit Corporation partnership, joint venture, trust, employee benefit plan, or other enterprise, against liability asserted against or incurred by him or her in that capacity or arising from his or her status as a Director, officer, employee, or agent, whether or not the Corporation would have power to indemnify the person against the same liability under section (A) or (B) above.

ARTICLE IX – AMENDMENTS TO ARTICLES AND BYLAWS

Any amendments to the Articles of Incorporation or the Corporation Bylaws must be approved by the Board of Directors.

(Name)

Incorporator

Your Notes

_____

_____

_____

_____

SAMPLE CLASS SURVEY

Beekeeping Class Survey   Date:_____

What did you think of the class? Please place a mark in the box that best reflects your answers and add comments for more details so we can make appropriate adjustments. Thank you!

QUESTIONS	5 GREAT	4 GOOD	3 OK	2 FAIR	1 POOR	COMMENTS
Did the class meet your expectations?						
Did you like the room?						
How were class materials?						
How could this class have been better?						
What other class topics would you be interested in?						
Any other comments?						

Your Name	Email	Phone Number	Hometown

SAMPLE CLUB CHARTER AGREEMENT

ARTICLE 1: NAME AND PURPOSE

Section 1: The name of the organization shall be Sample Bee Club at Samplebeeclub.com.

Section 2: Sample Bee Club was formed to increase public awareness of beekeeping; to support nonpartisan research and to educate beekeepers about beekeeping.

ARTICLE II: MEMBERSHIP

Section 3: No dues. There may be fees associated with classes and special events; the club will be run as a nonprofit corporation under its own employer identification number associated with (any sponsoring organizations)

Section 4: The Executive Committee shall have the authority to establish and define membership categories, class fees and any other fees associated with club management.

ARTICLE III: MEETINGS OF MEMBERS

Section 5: Monthly meetings shall be held at (day of month, time, address.) One or more of the Executive Board members will preside over the meetings.

Section 6: Special meetings may be called by any one of the Executive Board members.

ARTICLE IV: EXECUTIVE BOARD

Section 7: The Executive Board is responsible for overall policy and club direction.

Section 8: The Executive Board shall meet at least quarterly, at an agreed upon time and place, to plan the club's upcoming activities.

Section 9: There shall be three members of the Executive Board. The board will keep records, including overseeing the taking of minutes at meetings and assuring that corporate records are maintained. The board will work on training schedules for club meetings and meeting logistical support. Duties may be moved around board members at the board's discretion.

Section 10: One person shall make financial information available to the board.

Section 11: In the event the Executive Board disbands, the Executive Board members will dispose of all club equipment and assets in such a manner as not to benefit themselves individually but benefit other similar nonprofits.

ARTICLE V: AMENDMENTS

These charter bylaws may be amended by a majority of the Executive Board.

Approved: (Date) and signed by Executive Board members.

Your Notes

_____

_____

_____

_____

_____

_____

SAMPLE CODE OF CONDUCT

Volunteers are key partners, helping guide and deliver programs that matter to (state) citizens. The university depends and expects all volunteers to understand and uphold the following Volunteer Code of Conduct at all times while serving as a volunteer.

BE ACCOUNTABLE TO AND WORK WITHIN THE UNIVERSITY SYSTEM

1. Work within the scope of assigned volunteer role and follow all related program policies and procedures.

2. Conduct behavior in strict accordance with applicable laws and confidential information policies, using confidential information only as needed to perform volunteer duties. The following rules apply:

    a. access confidential information only with proper approval and refrain from misusing or treating it carelessly;

    b. do not divulge, copy, release, sell, loan, review, alter or destroy any confidential information except as properly authorized;

    c. understand and agree that any violation of the responsibilities explained in this section subjects a volunteer to discipline, possible removal from the volunteer role or legal liability.

What is meant by confidentiality? Confidential information means personal information of another person, which includes home addresses, telephone numbers, social security numbers, birth dates, etc. Also, do not include personal contact information of another in newsletters and announcements without their expressed consent.

3. Treat all youth and adults equally, without discrimination. This includes providing equal access to participation for all youth and adults, regardless of race, color, sex, pregnancy, national origin, ancestry, sexual orientation, gender identity, gender expression, religion, age, veteran status, disability, or any other status protected by applicable federal or state law. Sexual violence is also

prohibited, including but not limited to sexual misconduct, sexual exploitation, sex-based stalking, and dating/intimate partner violence.

4. Avoid harming youth or adults, whether through sexual harassment, physical force, verbal or mental abuse or neglect. Retaliation for making or supporting a report of discrimination or harassment is also prohibited.

5. If your volunteer responsibilities meet the definition of a mandated reporter (i.e. anyone with care, custody or control of a child), then assume the role of a mandated reporter and, if concerned a child has been/or will be abused and/or neglected, contact the child abuse hotline. If it appears the child is in imminent danger, contact law enforcement as well.

When am "I" a Mandated Reporter? If youth are registered participants in a program, you are responsible to report suspected symptoms of child abuse and neglect even if parents are present. Exception: When a school visits, the teacher in charge of the group is the mandated reporter.

6. Avoid conflict of interest between assigned volunteer role(s) and personal business interests.

BE A POSITIVE ROLE MODEL AT ALL TIMES

1. Obey all laws of the locality, state and nation, including laws against forgery, theft, destruction or defacement of property.

2. Display mutual respect to others, practicing patience, cooperation and teamwork.

3. Practice personal and intellectual integrity.

4. Under no circumstances engage in unlawful manufacture, distribution, dispensation, possession, or use of a controlled substance at any club event. Avoid unlawful possession, use and/or distribution of alcohol at any club event. Avoid misuse or abuse of prescribed or over-the-counter drugs.

5. Be respectful of diverse opinions and perspectives.

6. Actively promote a safe environment for participants, volunteers, visitors, staff and others involved in the program.

Please consider **volunteering as a privilege, not a right**. Adhering to the code of conduct ensures the safety and protection of all, including yourself. Additionally, you have the authority to report abuses of the code of conduct to your supervisor. Failure to uphold any of the code of conduct standards above may result in coaching by a supervisor. Depending on the severity, this may include reassignment, role restriction and, if appropriate, removal from all volunteer roles. As representatives of the club, we have a shared responsibility to watch out for one another and to ensure the code of conduct is being **followed.**

END SAMPLE CODE OF CONDUCT

Your Notes

_____

_____

_____

_____

_____

_____

_____

SAMPLE COVER COLORING PAGE

SAMPLE BEE CLUB EXPENSES ESTIMATE

EXPENSE	AMOUNT	THIS YEAR	NEXT YEAR	NOTES
Monthly Rent and Online Meeting Platform cost	$25* $15	(11 months) $275* $150	(11 months)	*possible rent increase next year
Coffee/Tea/Water Treats	$15	$165		
Business cards Chair rental	$25 $20	$25 $220		
Projector rental Computer rental	$10 $10	$110 $110		
Postage	$10	$110		
Name Tags	$5	$55		
Copies	$50	$50 One time		
Honey Tasting Awards	$25	$25		
Door Prizes	$50	$50		
Bee Club Basics Book bluebirdgardens.com/books	$34.95	(5 copies) $174.75		One for each officer and one to loan out
Subtotal GOAL for Next Year	-------	$1,410	$1,500	

SAMPLE GIFT CERTIFICATE

(Name of club/website)

Date_____

This gift certificate entitles _____

to a Beginning and/or Second Year beekeeping class at _____
in (date)_____.

Beginning classes (list dates)

To register, email (add email) and call (phone number)

_____

Certificate No. _____

(Signed) Club Officer

Your Notes

_____

_____

_____

_____

_____

SAMPLE MEETING AGENDA

A. Note date, time, location, who was in attendance.

B. STANDING REPORTS:

    Secretary: Last meeting's minutes

    Treasurer's report

C. OLD BUSINESS (pending items from past meetings)

    List a summary of the issue, who has details to share.

D. NEW BUSINESS (new topics)

E. STANDING COMMITTEE REPORTS

F. Next meeting (date, time, location)

Your Notes

_____

_____

_____

_____

_____

SAMPLE MEETING ROOM COMPARISON CHECK LIST

NAME & ADDRESS	RENT COST	PARKING	COFFEE POT	TOBACCO FREE	HANDICAP ACCESS	OTHER (HOURS)

SAMPLE MINOR PHOTO RELEASE FORM

I, _____, the parent or legal guardian of _____ [Child] grant _____ [Party Receiving Permission] my permission to use the photographs described as (describe photographs) _____ _____ for any legal use, including but not limited to: publicity, copyright purposes, illustration, advertising, and web content.

I understand that no royalty, fee or other compensation shall become payable to me by reason of such use.

Parent/Guardian's Signature: _____ Date _____

Parent/Guardian's Printed Name: _____

Child's Printed Name: _____

Parent's Phone Number: _____

Received by (Club Representative) _____

Date_____

_____

Keep in club record official files for future reference.

SAMPLE MEMORANDUM OF UNDERSTANDING

This Memorandum of Understanding (MOU) is entered into, by and between (list working partners) partners of the Missourians for Monarchs (Collaborative), working under the laws and authorities of (state) whose mission is (list mission.)

RESPONSIBILITIES OF WORKING PARTNERS

The working partners mutually agree to:

1. To support the goal(s) of_____
2. To work together by: (joint meetings, sharing assets, supporting an event(s)
3. To annually the progress towards the mutually-agreed upon goal(s).
4. If there are financial contributions, those are usually covered in a separate document.
5. This working partnership will continue until _____ and/or be renewed (ie. annually)
6. Signatures and dates of each party representative.
7. List of working parties and their representatives.

SAMPLE MONTHLY CLUB PROGRAMS

MONTH	TOPIC	SPEAKER	NOTES	EQUIPMENT/ SUPPLIES NEEDED
January	How to winter feed Planting for Pollinators Making wax frames			
February	Pollen feeding Repairing frames/painting Pros and cons of buying Beginning beekeeping kits Winter Spring Turnover			
March	Signs of Swarm preparation Catching swarms Package Installation Spring inspections			
April	Upcoming nectar flow How to start smoker Raising queens			

MONTH	TOPIC	SPEAKER	NOTES	EQUIPMENT/ SUPPLIES NEEDED
May	How to mark queen Sugar water feeding *Varroa* powdered sugar roll *Varroa* alcohol wash Planting for pollinators May 20 World Bee Day			
June	How to raise queens Swarm prevention Monitoring colony growth			
July	End of nectar flow Signs of robbing *Varroa* management options			
August	How to winterize hives Oxalic acid vapor and dribble How to make sugar board Honey extracting			
September	Winter bees Winterizing hives Fall planting			

SAMPLE CHECK LISTS AND DOCUMENTS

MONTH	TOPIC	SPEAKER	NOTES	EQUIPMENT/ SUPPLIES NEEDED
October	Annual honey taste contest How to clean smoker Winter reading			
November	Bee ordering options Pros and cons of packages Winter feeding			
December	Celebrate the year			
January				
Notes:				

SAMPLE MONTHLY MEETING CALENDARS

	BEE CLUB MONTHLY TOPICS CALENDAR: JANUARY			
Check off	Topic	Speaker	Need	Notes
	Welcome New Year's Resolutions	All		
	Winter feeding			
	February Pollen feeding			
	Making wax frames and woodenware			
	Other:			

BEE CLUB MONTHLY TOPICS CALENDAR: FEBRUARY

Check Off	Topic	Speaker	Need	Notes
	Welcome Bees as Nature's Matchmakers			
	Late winter Feeding; how are bees so far	All		
	Planting For Pollinators			
	What are you planting for your bees?	All		
	Understanding Pollen			
	Hive Repairs			
	Spring Build up			
	Other:			

BEE CLUB MONTHLY TOPICS CALENDAR: MARCH

Check Off	Topic	Speaker	Need	Notes
	Welcome Spring			
	How are your bees?	All		
	Preparing for the Nectar Flow			
	Varroa Management plan			
	Spring Inspections			
	Locating Hives			
	Other:			

BEE CLUB MONTHLY TOPICS CALENDAR: APRIL

Check Off	Topic	Speaker	Need	Notes
	Welcome Swarm Monitoring	All		
	Spring Nectar Flow Projections			
	How to Re-queen			
	Drone removal for *Varroa* management			
	Nuc Care Tips			
	Package Installation			
	How to Manage Smoker			
	Other:			

BEE CLUB MONTHLY TOPICS CALENDAR: MAY

Check Off	Topic	Speaker	Need	Notes
	Welcome / Happy Mother's Day / May 20 World Bee Day			
	Managing Nectar Flow			
	Marking queens (with Drones)	All		
	Catching Swarms			
	Feeding Nucs			
	Other:			

BEE CLUB MONTHLY TOPICS CALENDAR: JUNE

Check Off	Topic	Speaker	Need	Notes
	Welcome Happy Father's Day			
	End of Nectar Flow			
	Making Splits			
	Honey Production Estimates	All		
	Feeding Nucs			
	Varroa Management			
	Other:			

BEE CLUB MONTHLY TOPICS CALENDAR: JULY

Check Off	Topic	Speaker	Need	Notes
	Welcome Happy 4th!			
	Honey Extracting	All		
	Varroa Management			
	Supplemental Feeding			
	Winter Prep			
	Other:			

BEE CLUB MONTHLY TOPICS CALENDAR: AUGUST

Check Off	Topic	Speaker	Need	Notes
	Welcome Back to School			
	Impacts of Dearth	All		
	Fall Nectar Flow and Feeding			
	Signs of Robbing			
	Varroa Management			
	Other:			

BEE CLUB MONTHLY TOPICS CALENDAR: SEPTEMBER

Check Off	Topic	Speaker	Need	Notes
	Welcome Fall			
	Fall Nectar Flow	All		
	Planting For Pollinators			
	Varroa Management			
	Supplemental Winter Feeding			
	Other:			

BEE CLUB MONTHLY TOPICS CALENDAR: OCTOBER

Check Off	Topic	Speaker	Need	Notes
	Welcome Trick or Treat			
	Hive Repairs			
	How to Store Frames and Equipment			
	Winter Prep	All		
	Other:			

BEE CLUB MONTHLY TOPICS CALENDAR: NOVEMBER				
Check Off	Topic	Speaker	Need	Notes
	Welcome Happy Thanksgiving			
	Winter Feeding			
	What worked well this past year	All		
	Varroa management: Oxalic Acid			
	Ordering Bees			
	Other:			

SAMPLE PLANNING GOALS

WHAT YOU WANT TO DO, HOW DO YOU PLAN TO DO IT				
	GOAL 1	GOAL 2	GOAL 3	NOTES
Describe goals				
How to implement				
What action				
Why desired result(s)?				
By whom (name) someone responsible				
What needed (list supplies/actions)				
By when (set a goal date)				
What happens if goal not met (describe impact)				
Other needed measurable steps				

SAMPLE BEE CLUB NEWS RELEASE

From Sample Bee Club

Address

Phone Number

Email and website

REGISTRATION OPEN FOR JANUARY 27, 2018 BASIC BEEKEEPING CLASS

Hometown, State, -- Registration is now open for a basic beekeeping class (Day/Date/Location/Address/Time)

Cost $$ per person including lunch and class materials. Class size is limited; attendees must be at least 15 years of age or older. To register, send your name, email and phone number to SAMPLE EMAIL and a check to TREASURER **no later than (SPECIFY DATE)**

The basic beekeeping classes will include sample sample sample.

Instructors are active beekeepers

For more information about Sample Bee Club, visit samplebeeclub.com.

-end—

Your Notes

_____

_____

_____

SAMPLE NEWSLETTER GUIDELINES

What is the newsletter objective? Newsletters should revolve around your club objectives and what **you want members to know.** Include newsletter content that is **relevant, helpful and interesting:**

1. **Latest news,** ie. Passage of bees classified as livestock and no longer taxed.
2. **Industry developments**, ie. Frank's bees move to Smalltown. Nancy's Ice Cream expands distribution route.
3. **Frequently-asked questions.**
4. **"How to" articles.**
5. **Upcoming conference** highlights:
   a. Short stories on upcoming **conference keynote speakers.**
   b. **Info on contests:** honey, cooking, etc.
   c. Short description of location and community where conference will be held.
   d. **Recognize** volunteers helping with the event.
6. **Feature stories about members.** If you have awards, have **feature stories about award nominees**, then follow-up with stories about winners.
7. **Upcoming** classes/events/feature stories.
8. In general,
   a. **Keep feature stories** between 400-500 words. Other articles 200-300 words.
   b. **Ask for** both horizontal and vertical photos per feature story; two of each so editor has some choices. Sizing no less than 300 dpi and originals, not photoshopped.
   c. Include one or two **calls to action:** volunteer to help, join the club.
   d. Consider **photo feature page** featuring an event or activity.
   e. Add **letters to the editor** section to get leads on story ideas.

SAMPLE OFFICER JOB DESCRIPTIONS

PRESIDENT

The president has the **long-range view,** making sure the club is headed in the right direction. The president often tweaks the club's mission based on past successes and future goals all designed to support the club's main mission.

- The focus of this position is to find good people and to make sure the others **are working out well in their positions and with each other.**
- **The president has the organization's best interests in mind, not his/her interests.** Even if the president doesn't like legalities or details, the president follows the laws and checks details because this is now about making sure the club is working well. Most groups need both policies and procedures to work smoothly.

The most important selection this person makes is the vice president, who often succeeds the president.

VICE PRESIDENT

Most vice presidents focus on the **day-to-day operations**, making sure deadlines get met, required reports get filed and conflicts get quickly resolved.

- This is the position with the short-term view, focused on **keeping momentum going.**
- It's also an excellent position to train for the presidency because this person develops an understanding of the mission and knows how the club operates.

It is critical for the **president and vice president to work closely together** since they both bring something different but complimentary to the club.

However, people who are used to tracking details can be challenged to move into the "longer range" presidential position because they are no longer in charge of the details and have to depend on others to get the work done. **If this leadership team can sort out what needs to be done and divide the workload among themselves, that can work, too.**

SECRETARY

The secretary is the one who **keeps the club records** from meeting notes to historic files and documents.

- This can be an easy job if the **person running the meeting** runs the meeting well and decisions are clearly stated and understood. However, if the person running the meeting doesn't follow the meeting agenda or clearly manages how decisions are made, this can be a very challenging position. It can open the club up to political gamesmanship as members try to alter previous decisions they don't support.
- The best defense is to have **good job descriptions** and **clear notes.**

TREASURER

The treasurer is the **money person**, collecting and making payments while **keeping records** of how the money came in and was spent. A good treasurer will

- **Prepare budgets** showing planned expenditures and estimates
- **Show expenses** over time,
- Note when something is **out of the ordinary** and
- **Make recommendations** for good money stewardship.

PAST PRESIDENT

Whenever I am thinking of volunteering at an organization, this is one of the people I contact with my questions. The past president is **the mentor** for the incoming vice president and president. This person can be **most influential** because of established relationships and knowledge picked up in earlier positions.

SAMPLE SIGN-UP SHEET

Thanks for signing up to get information about a possible local bee club. Your email will only be used to send meeting and other pertinent bee club information. For more details, contact (Name, phone number, email)

	NAME	ADDRESS	PHONE NUMBER	EMAIL
1.	B. Queen	100 Hive Drive, Bee Town	555-333-8889	4queen@bmail.com
2.				
3.				
4.				
5.				
6.				
7.				
8.				
9.				
10.				
11.				
12.				

SAMPLE CLUB VOLUNTEER JOBS CHECK LIST

☐ Bee Wranglers

Name: _____

Start/End Dates: _____

☐ Club Ambassadors

Name: _____

Start/End Dates: _____

☐ Communications

Name: _____

Start/End Dates: _____

☐ Community Relations

Name: _____

Start/End Dates: _____

☐ Fundraisers

Name: _____

Start/End Dates: _____

☐ Greeters

Name: _____

Start/End Dates: _____

☐ Medical Support

Name: _____

Start/End Dates: _____

☐ Meeting Logistics

Name: _____

Start/End Dates: _____

☐ Membership

Name: _____

Start/End Dates: _____

☐ Military Liaison

Name: _____

Start/End Dates: _____

☐ Newsletter Editor and Co-Editor

Name: _____

Start/End Dates: _____

☐ Partnership Liaison

Name: _____

Start/End Dates: _____

☐ Photographer

Name: _____

Start/End Dates: _____

☐ Program Chair

Name: _____

Start/End Dates: _____

☐ Refreshments

Name: _____

Start/End Dates: _____

☐ Security

Name: _____

Start/End Dates: _____

☐ Special Events Coordinators

Name: _____

Start/End Dates: _____

☐ Tech Support

Name: _____

Start/End Dates: _____

☐ Volunteer Recruiter

Name: _____

Start/End Dates: _____

☐ Webmaster

Name: _____

Start/End Dates: _____

About the Author

Charlotte Ekker Wiggins was elected to her local city council 1999-2007 and has helped to establish more than a dozen educational nonprofits. She started in 1979 establishing a county humane society.

Charlotte has a master's degree in management from Webster University, St. Louis. She is also a Great Plains Master Beekeeping Program Certified Master Beekeeper with the University of Nebraska at Lincoln. As a University of Missouri Master Gardener Emeritus, she helped to develop Missouri's Master Pollinator Steward Program as a contributing author and Steering Committee member: https://bit.ly/MPS-program.

In 2019, she was selected by Missouri S&T to do a TEDx talk on "Why Bugs Matter."

https://bit.ly/WhyBugsMatter

Charlotte has also served as the Heroes to Hives Missouri chapter military advisor, the first chapter in a nationwide program to help military veterans and their families learn beekeeping. She also volunteered as Missouri State Beekeepers Association's partnership liaison.

In 2014, she started what is now an educational nonprofit bee club to support her students.

Charlotte has kept honey bees since 2010. She retired from public affairs careers in US Navy in 2009 and the US Forest Service in 2015. Also in 2015, she was selected Missouri State Beekeepers Association Beekeeper of the Year along with a team of other volunteers who changed Missouri's honey labeling laws.

She lives with rescue cats on a one-acre Missouri garden. The limestone hillside, where neighbors said nothing would ever grow, is now a certified wildlife habitat, Monarch Way Station and working apiary that inspires her custom gift business Bluebird Gardens.

And for the record, Charlotte doesn't drink coffee.

Charlotte does frequently lecture on planting for pollinators and how to start a bee club. For more details, visit charlotteekkerwiggins.com and email 4charlottewiggins@gmail.com.

Other Published Works

"A Beekeeper's Diary, Self-Guide to Beekeeping" 2nd Edition, December 2021 in paperback and eBook (70% in color). The definitive guide on to how to start keeping bees with handy checklists and guides.

https://www.charlotteekkerwiggins.com/a-beekeepers-diary-book.html

"Bee Club Basics or How to Start a Bee Club" first edition published October 2019.

https://www.charlotteekkerwiggins.com/bee-club-basics-book.html

COMING NEXT:

"Bees Need Flowers, Planting for Pollinators" 2023. How to assess your current property's ability to feed your bees and how to provide bees, and other pollinators, with healthy food sources.

https://www.charlotteekkerwiggins.com/bees-need-flowers-book.html

FREE WEEKLY NEWSLETTER

Sign up for her free **Garden Notes,** Charlotte's weekly email on gardening, beekeeping, cooking, easy home décor and nature: http://eepurl.com/cwzx_z

Charlotte frequently blogs at these sites:

http://www.Gardeningcharlotte.com, tips on USDA Hardiness zone 5 gardening.

http://www.Homesweetbees.com, beekeeping tips.

http://www.Ateaspoon.com, food facts and favorite easy recipes.

http://www.Madejustforu.com, custom personalized quilts, gifts and easy home décor ideas.

She has also been a contributing writer to American Bee Journal, Bee Culture, 2 Million Blossoms Magazines and a regular contributing writer to Missouri Gardener Magazine for 6 years. She was syndicated through newspapers with a weekly gardening, beekeeping and cooking column for 8 years. For other writing samples, visit https://www.charlotteekkerwiggins.com/writing-samples.html

Charlotte Ekker Wiggins has been gardening on this Missouri limestone hillside since 1982, where neighbors said nothing would grow. She added honey bees in 2010. She has been growing dozens of dwarf and semi-dwarf fruit trees **with the pollination help** *of her bees.*

Your Notes

Glossary of Terms

American Bee Journal: Monthly publication by Dadant and Sons on beekeeping-related topics.

Apiary: Where beekepers keep their bees. Also referred to as a bee garden.

Apis mellifera – Latin for European honey bee, the most common of the 7-12 worldwide honey bee species.

Awards: A way to recognize volunteers for thei contributions and to reinforce desirable qualities and behavior.

Articles of Incorporation: The document that establishes a club and organization as a separate, distinct legal entity.

Backfire: To have the opposite of the desired effect.

Background Checks: Process to verify than an individual is who they claim to be and to confirm the validity of someone's criminal record, education, employment history and other past activities.

Bad Conduct: Unacceptable behavior outlined in written codes of conduct.

Bee (s): European honey bee *Apis mellifera*.

Bee Buddy: Someone who starts keeping bees when you do, is usually close to where you live and who enjoys sharing information, visiting each other's apiaries and learning together.

Bee Check: Missouri's voluntary hive location registration.

Bee Culture Magazine: Monthly beekeeping publication published by John Root.

Bee Math: Knowing how long things should take to help beekeepers predict where development are going and/or where things have been.

Beekeeping Etiquette: Good beekeeping practices with neighbors and helpful beekeepers.

Best Management Practices: How to get things effectively done to achieve optimal results.

Board: Short for Board of Directors.

Burnout: State of emotional, physical and mental exhausting caused by excessive and prolonged stress.

Bylaws: Rules and regulations designed to regulate the actions of a club and organization's members.

Calling Tree: Also called a phone tree, is defined as **a pyramid-shaped method of communication** which is started by one person and is continued as each contact receives the message and relays it to another group member.

Certified Master Beekeeper: Beekeepers who have completed either exams or educational programs to establish their extent of beekeeping knowledge.

Certified Public Accountant: Someone licensed in your state to provide accounting services to the public.

Club: A group of individuals who are focused on sharing information and supporting each other.

Club Charter: Basic operational guidelines for a beginning club that include minimum legal requirements, the foundation of bylaws.

Code of Conduct: A list of expectations of how program participants are expected to behave.

Conflict of Interest: A situation in which the concerns or aims of two different parties are incompatible or a situation in which a person is in a position to derive personal benefit from actions or decisions made in their official capacity.

COVID: Short for COVID-19, a coronavirus called SARS-CoV-2 that spreads mainly through person-to-person contact and triggered a worldwide pandemic that started in the US March 2020 with a nationwide quarantine.

Delta variant: The delta variant is a SARS-CoV2 strain and first detected in the US March 2021.

GLOSSARY

Email List: Consolidated list of everyone who has given you permission to contact them for a specific purpose only.

Employer Identification Number (EIN) Internal Revenue Service-issued number akin to a driver's license and social security identification number for a club or organization.

Executive Committee: The club's legal leadership comprising of president, vice president, secretary and/or treasurer and sometimes past president.

Facebook Group Page: One of the social media platform's options to easily allow people to share photos, videos and other information.

Financial Structures: How clubs organize to generate money to operate.

For Profit: The club or organization makes money that benefits the club owners.

Forage: When bees search widely for food, usually a 2-mile radius from their home colony.

Formal Contracts: Legally-binding documents outlining what each participant agrees to do and what happens if they don't.

Fun: Collective enjoyable activities that keep people coming back for more. And if you had to look this word up, you need to reconsider what you're doing!

Gift Certificates: Pre-paid funds to cover a class expense and/or item purchase offered by a club.

Giveaways: Items that are purchased or donated by the club to give to club members.

GoFundMe: An online fundraising platform.

Great Plains Master Beekeeping Program: An educational master beekeeping program out of the University of Nebraska at Lincoln.

Heroes to Hives: Beginning beekeeping program launched by the University of Michigan to teach military veterans and their immediate family members nationwide how to keep bees.

Holiday Dinners: There are a number of special days in the US considered holidays including Memorial Day, Fourth of July, Labor Day, Thanksgiving and Christmas among others.

Informal Contracts: Agreements between parties outlining what each of the participants will do.

Honey Bee: European honey bee *Apis mellifera*.

IRS: Internal Revenue Service, a US government agency responsible for giving specific tax-exempt designations and nonprofit status to groups.

Job Description: Itemized duties expected to be completed by the person in that position.

Lawyer: Someone licensed in your state to practice law.

Leadership: Individuals legally responsible for the direction and day to day operations of a club.

Local Extension Offices: Most universities have outreach branches called extensions where experts support public education programs.

Mail Chimp: Email list management platform.

Master Candidate: Great Plains Master Beekeeping candidate for certified master beekeeper.

Master Gardeners: University trained volunteer gardeners who educate others about gardening.

Master Naturalists: Missouri Department of Conservation-trained volunteer landowners taught to restore Missouri's plant communities.

Memorandums of Understanding: Written, non-legally binding documents outlining what each participant has agreed to do.

Mentor: Experienced beekeeper who takes a less experienced beekeeper under their wing, answers questions, takes them out to work apiaries and engages the beekeeper with hands on experience.

Missouri Master Pollinator Steward Program: A five-course educational outreach program developed through University of Missouri's School of Natural Resources to teach the public about the value and role of pollinators.

Monthly Topics Calendar: Proposed topics for speakers, presentations, discussions and hands on club activities.

MSBA: Missouri State Beekeepers Association.

GLOSSARY

My Math: Tongue-in-check but not far from the truth cost of my first jar of honey.

Newbee: Someone just starting to learn to keep bees, usually 1-3 years depending on how much effort they apply and how much they learn.

Nonprofit: The club or organization makes money that benefits the club or organization, not the club members or leaders.

Noxious Weeds: Legal definition that sometimes confuses wildflowers with undesirable plants that are excellent pollinator food.

Partnership Liaison: A volunteer club position helping to connect with other groups with similar goals.

Provisional Journeyman: Great Plains Master Beekeeping program designation of their master beekeeping program's educational levels with requirements to complete volunteer hours and written and hands on testing to move from Apprentice Level to the next education level.

On the Books: Contained in a book of laws or formal records.

Open Apiary: Apiary that is open to beekeepers to work hands on with bees.

Planning Team: The precursor to a club's executive committee.

Practicing Beekeeper: Beekeepers who have successfully been keeping bees including pulling colonies through winter and using the basic beekeeping skills of splitting, re-queening, making nucleus colonies and managing for pests and diseases.

Personal Benefit: When someone gets a benefit greater than he or she provides a group; prohibited in all nonprofits and one of two potential conflicts of interest.

Pollinators: animals that move pollen from the male flower anther to the female flower stigma ensuring the propagation of the plant. 80% of all pollinators are bees followed by hummingbirds, butterflies and flies.

Online Meeting Platforms: Online services that facilitate online meetings.

Queen(s): Short for queen honey bee.

Red Clover: *Trifolium pretense*, a type of clover that bumblebees can easily access but not honey bees.

Red Crimson Clover: *Trifolium incarnatum,* which provides early spring nitrogen as a cover crop, helps recondition soil and is an excellent honey bee nectar and pollen source.

Refreshments: Usually a variety of drinks and food to share.

Robert's Rules of Order: Set of **rules** first published in 1876 by Henry M. Robert to run orderly meetings with maximum fairness to all members. Considered the current standard for meeting management.

Round Robin: Going around the room and invite every person to speak on a specified topic.

Safety Briefing: Informal safety meeting generally conducted at a meeting and/or job site prior to the commencement of a job or work shift. Event supervisors draw attention to hazards, processes, equipment, tools, environment and materials to inform all workers of the risks in their surroundings.

Safety Precautions: A series of reminders and review of practices prior to execution to ensure all participants are unharmed.

Self-Dealing: Working both sides of a transaction resulting in a conflict of interest.

Show and Tell: When participants bring items to describe and share with other club members.

Social Hour: Informal gathering period so people can talk and share stories and a cup of coffee.

Social Media: Online platforms used to market information.

Start Up Funds: Usually a one-time source of funding.

Succession Planning: How volunteers fill and move through positions to ensure the club's organizational continuity.

Superorganism: Synergistically interacting same species organisms.

Swarm Lists: Some clubs offer lists of beekeepers willing to take calls to collect bee swarms.

Taxon: A taxonomic group of any rank, such as a species family or class.

TEDx: Independently-organized lectures focused on local community issues. More info at TED.com.

Value of Volunteer Time: University of Maryland's Do Good Institute calculates the annual value of volunteer time based on US Bureau of Labor Statistics hourly earnings.

Vendor Coordinator: A club member working with businesses interested in a space at your event to share information and/or sell items.

White Elephant Exchange: Gift exchange where participants donate an item, draw numbers and those with numbers select a gift to open or take an already opened gift, leaving the gift recipient to select a replacement gift. For time's sake, only allow one gift taking or this event could go on for days! When planning giveways, remember to include both **beekeeping and flower-related items** to remind beekeepers to feed their bees with healthy plants.

Your Notes

Index

A

Adam, Brother quote, 189

Alcott, Louisa May quote, 169

Alcohol, 63, 87, 202, 226

Alternatives to Robert's Rules of Order, 56, 73, 215

American Bee Journal, 195, 261

Annual Volunteer Code of Conduct, 85

Appearance of Conflict of Interest, 85

Arts and Crafts Contests, 112

Awards Examples, 181–182

Awards Program, 180

B

Background Checks, 80, 193

Bad Conduct, 85

Bake Sales, 112

Baking Contests, 113

Basic Bee Club Financial Structures, 24–26

Bee Buddy, xi, vi, 41, 93–96, 111–114, 160, 185

Bee Check, 165

Bee Club Charter, 19, 51

Bee Club Meeting Notice, 151, 208

Bee Club Membership Dues, 24

Bee Club Newsletter, 142

Bee Club Planning Team, 32-34

Bee Culture Magazine, 11, 161, 195

Best Friends, 13, 22

Bee Math, 106

Bee-Related Special Days, 76

Beginning Beekeeping Class Agenda, 115

Beginning Beekeeping Class Survey, 116, 210

Beekeeping Etiquette, 97

Beepods Trivia, 14, 22, 30, 44, 64, 82, 88, 100, 110, 138, 154, 169, 168, 180, 190, 198

Being Queen, 67

Benefit Auctions, 150

Best Management Practices, 7–11, 95, 97, 105

Board of Directors, 18, 54–62

Book Sales, 116

Burham, Toni quote, 161

Burlew, Rusty quote, 24

Business Cards, 29, 45, 229

Business Club Sponsor, 12–13

C

Calling Tree, 160

Changing Laws, 161

Charitable Educational Nonprofit, 12

Certification Beekeeping Programs, 95

Certified Master Beekeepers, 95

Certified Public Accountant, 13, 19, 22

Coaches, 10, 40, 95, 114

Code of Conduct, 85-88, 201, 225

Coffee, 1, 3-4, 15-16, 23, 26, 29, 34, 36-38, 41, 63, 92, 96, 141, 185, 199, 229, 232, 258

Colopy, Michele, viii, 189, 194

Conflict of Interest, viii, 58, 80, 83-85, 87, 192, 202, 217, 226,

COVID, 37, 91, 114, 155, 160

Corporate Giving Program, 21

Cover Coloring Page, 228

Club Charter Agreement, 46, 223

Club Name, 33, 48

Club Volunteer Jobs Check List, 99-100, 255-256

D

Darwin, Charles quote, 31

Dickinson, Emily quote, 1

Did You Know, 14, 22, 30, 44, 64, 82, 88, 100, 110, 138, 154, 160, 168, 176, 188, 198

Dinners, 119

Donate Books, 81

Donations, 13, 20-21, 24-25, 27, 33-35, 37, 106, 150-151, 156, 177, 190, 208

Do's and Dont's of Social Media, 144-145

Dues, 24, 47, 151, 208, 223

Draker, David quote, 111

E

Education Programs, 95

Email Lists, 139-142, 149

Employer Identification Number, 18, 47, 223

Entomology Society of America, 3

Equipment Sales, 117

Executive Committee, 33, 47, 70, 174, 182, 191, 223

Exit Strategy, 178

Expenses, 23-29, 35, 51, 59-60, 63, 80, 174, 217-219, 229, 253

F

Facebook Groups, 33, 146-147

Facebook Policy, 145

Financial Structures, 24

Finding Speakers, 105

Formal Knowledge, 183

Frequently-Asked Questions, 105, 152, 189, 190-193, 251

Fundraising Challenges, 79

Funding Options, 31

INDEX

G

Garden Visits, 117

Getting the Word Out, 139

Gift Certificates, 117–118, 230

Giveaways, 40, 120

Great Plains Master Beekeeping, ix, 95, 185, 257

H

Heroes to Hives, 120, 196, 257

Hive Products, 23, 96, 106, 112

Holiday Dinners, 119

Honey Extracting, 103, 108, 236

Honey Lemon Cake Recipe, 187

Honey Tasting Contest, 93, 119, 182

How Best to Stay In Touch, 1, 140

How Decisions are Made, 73

Hubbell, Sue quote, 101

K

Kidd, Sue Monk quote, 65

L

Lawyer, 13, 22, 32, 48, 52, 161, 163, 189, 194

LEAD for Pollinators, vi, 81, 189, 191, 194

Leadership, 65–71, 83–84, 97, 169, 178, 181–186, 190–191, 194, 252

Leadership Challenges, 78–81

Liability Insurance, 80–81, 122

Liability Waivers, 176

Local Ordinances, 9, 163

M

Managing Volunteers, 89–100

Mandated Reporter, 86–87

Maeterlinck, Maurice quote, 139, 149

Medical Advice, 154

Meeting Online, 3, 16, 38, 155

Meeting Places, 35–37

Meeting Planning, 3, 74, 76, 156

Meeting Review, 42

Meeting Site, 36

Meeting Topics, 74

Memberships, 10, 22, 24–25, 47, 92, 100, 174, 223, 255

Memorandum of Understanding, 172, 234

Mentors, 8, 10, 70, 93–94, 113, 115, 177, 181, 209, 253, 264

Military Liaison, 92, 100, 173, 255

Military Veterans Programs, 120

Missouri Master Pollinator Steward Program, 121, 264

MSBA Best Management Practices, 7–10

Monthly Meeting Planning Check List, 76–77

Monthly Programs Topics Calendar, 102–104, 107–109, 125–136

N

Name Tags, 29, 96, 113, 229

Newbee, 93, 265

Newsletter Ideas, 142

Newsletter Topics, 142-143

Nonprofit Club Types, 20-22

Not-For-Profit, 22

Noxious Weeds, 124, 265

Nuc Sales, 113

O

Online Meeting, 3, 26, 29, 34, 77, 91-92, 155-160, 229

Online Meeting Platforms, 156, 265

On-the-Job Experience, 183

P

Partners, 11, 16, 29, 121, 169-175, 234

Partnerships, 29, 169-175

Partnership Liaison, 92, 100, 173-175, 257, 265

Patches, 25, 80

Personal Benefit, 84, 262

Photo Release Form, 153, 233

Photography Contests, 122

Planning Team, viii, 4, 32-34, 45-46, 51, 63, 78-79, 141, 191, 265

Planting for Pollinators, 102, 104, 107-108, 122, 124, 134, 235-236, 258

President, 33, 45, 54-58, 63, 68-74, 78, 91, 178, 182, 185, 213, 215-217, 252

Practicing Beekeeper, 95, 97, 265

Private Charitable Foundation, 21

Proverbs 16:24 quote, 89

Purpose of Bee Club, 2

Q

Queen Bee Sales, 113

Quinn, Jane Bryant quote, 83

R

Recognition Awards, 180

References, 3, 61, 189, 195, 220

Refreshments, 26, 38, 77, 91-92, 100, 151, 208, 256

Re-Invigorating Existing Club, 32

Retaining Volunteers, 97-99

Retirement, 177, 181, 184, 192

Roosevelt, Eleanor quote, 45

RollaBeeClub.com, viii

Running a Meeting, 71

S

Sample Articles of Incorporation, 48

Sample Basic Meeting Agenda, 72

Sample Bee Club Expenses Estimate, 29

Sample Bee Club Goals, 207

INDEX

Sample Bee Club Meeting Notices, 151, 208

Sample Beginning Class Agenda, 209

Sample Best Management Practices, 7-10

Sample Bylaws, 52-62, 211-221

Sample Class Survey, 116, 222

Sample Club Charter Agreement, 46, 223

Sample Club Expenses, 29, 229

Sample Club Meeting Notices, 137, 151, 208

Sample Club Meeting Topics, 125-136, 238-248

Sample Code of Conduct, 86-88, 225-227

Sample Gift Certificate, 118, 230

Sample Meeting Agenda, 72, 231

Sample Meeting Room Comparison Check List, 36, 232

Sample Minor Photo Release Form, 153, 233

Sample Memorandum of Understanding, 172, 234

Sample Monthly Club Programs, 102-104, 235-248

Sample Monthly Meeting Planning Check List, 76-77

Sample Planning Chart, 6

Sample News Release, 151, 250

Sample Newsletter Guidelines, 152, 251

Sample Officer Job Descriptions, 252

Sample Partnership Liaison, 174

Sample Sign Up Sheet, 17, 254

Sample Thank You Note, 99

Sample Volunteer Code of Conduct, 86, 201

Sample Volunteer Jobs Check List, 99, 255-256

Self-Dealing, 84, 192, 266

Shakespeare, William quote, 199

Secretary, 20, 33, 46, 50, 54-58, 69-74, 170, 182, 189, 195, 199, 205, 213-217, 231, 253, 263

Selling Items, 25, 80

Show and Tell, 40-41, 89, 102, 266

Social Advocacy Nonprofit, 21

Social Hour, 38, 41, 266

Social Media, 33, 74, 120, 144, 149, 182, 266

Social Welfare Nonprofit, 21

Speaker Frequently-Asked Questions, 105-106

Special Club Events, 111-136

Special Privileges, 79-80

Statista Trivia, 64

Start Up Funds, 266

Steiner, Achim quote, 177

Swarm Lists, 122, 266

Succession Planning, 70, 266

Superorganism, 4, 266

T

Table Signs, 96

Thank You, 65, 96, 98-99, 106, 181, 185, 199

Teachers, 10, 114

TEDx, vi, 186, 196, 257

Tips, 42, 103, 241, 259

Tolstoy, Leo quote, 15

Treasurer, 33, 49, 56–58, 70–74, 78–79, 151, 204, 215–217, 231, 250, 253, 266

T-Shirts, 25, 80

V

Vendor Coordinator, 175, 266

Vice President, 56, 69, 215, 252–253

Volunteers, 31, 33, 41–42, 65–66, 70–71, 85–86, 89–91, 97–98, 112–113, 125, 147, 151–152, 175, 179, 191, 199, 201, 208, 225, 251, 257

Volunteer Hourly Value, 84

Volunteer Jobs, 99, 255

Volunteer Jobs Check List, 99, 255

Volunteer Turn Over, 98

Von Furstenberg, Diane quote, 155

W

Website, 28, 76, 90, 93, 98, 105, 118–123, 140, 143, 146, 149–151, 195, 230, 250

White Elephant Exchange, 125, 267

Working Partners, 169–175

Working Partners Charter, 173

Working with Kids, 80

Your Notes

Not the end but the beginning of your beekeeping club adventures!

www.ingramcontent.com/pod-product-compliance
Lightning Source LLC
Chambersburg PA
CBHW081707100526
44590CB00022B/3692